HISTORIC HAUNTS FLORIDA II

JAMIE ROUSH PEARCE

THE THIRD BOOK IN THE
HISTORIC HAUNTS SERIES

Inquiries should be addressed to:

Jamie Roush
historichaunts@yahoo.com

Foreword:

In this book I tried to include any and all personal experiences I had at each of the locations I've written about. Unfortunately, ghosts, as I like to say, do not perform on cue. In situations where my personal experiences were limited, I tried to interview people who lived or worked at the locations, past or present. Hours of research, traveling to the different locations, visiting, investigating, touring, and interviewing, all went into writing this book and I loved every moment of it! I have heard a lot of fascinating stories, experienced a lot of paranormal activity, and have made new friends. I look forward to starting on the next volume of Historic Haunts.

Dedications and Acknowledgements:

First I want to thank my amazing husband for all his hard work on getting this book ready and being part of so many of the investigations. Without you in my life I wouldn't be the person I am today. I love you, Deric. XOXO

I also want to thank two of my dear friends, Eric and Jolyn O'Dierno, who are also part of my Historic Haunts Investigations team. I am so thankful the paranormal brought us together and we have such an awesome friendship. I love you guys.

Also, I want to thank Florida Fringe Tourism for some great historic and haunted locations I may have never learned about without their website.
www.floridafringetourism.com

Finally, I want to say, seeing Vincent Price in "House on Haunted Hill" at a VERY early age also peaked my interested in the paranormal. I grew up looking up to Uncle Vinny and he is one of the people who inspired my passion for the field.
Also, Edgar Allan Poe inspired me to write about such a fascinating subject and without his work, I may not have started writing about my experiences.

Special Thanks:

Editing: Deric Pearce & Paula Dillon

Design and Layout: Deric Pearce
All Photographs are copyright the author or credited to their photographers
Additional photography provided by and copyright Big Stock

First Printing August 2014

HISTORIC HAUNTS FLORIDA

Table of Contents

3

IRISH CLASS AND SPECTRAL SASS
Culhane's Irish Pub, Atlantic Beach, Florida

Culhane's front entrance

Making the Irish American Dream

Once upon a time four members of a large Irish family had a dream. These four sisters Mary Jane, Aine, Lynda, and Michelle moved to the United States to Atlantic Beach and tried to make their American dream come true. They pooled their resources, emptied their savings accounts and piggy banks, and began to build an Irish Pub. With the help of family members from Ireland pitching in to do carpentry and other work, and friends lending advice, aid, and a helping hand, Culhane's Irish Pub opened its doors in 2005. Since then this Irish Publick House has come into its own. It offers a comfortable family environment unlike anything else in Jacksonville (perhaps because it was built by family) and its food has made it a diehard favorite of locals in the Atlantic Beach area and all over Jacksonville. So much so, in fact, that it drew the attention of Guy Fieri and was featured on his "Diners, Drive-Ins, and Dives" television show.

This gorgeous Irish Pub not only has awesome food, four fabulous sisters running it and a great atmosphere, it also has a resident ghost.

The Story of the Resident Ghost

You could refer to the spirit here as Casper, because this ghost is very friendly. We will refer to her as Barbara since her family resides in the area. Barbara was the restaurant manager and loved by all. She was like family to the sisters and the staff and always worried about everyone else before herself.

On Christmas Eve 2010 Barbara was hit by a car and rushed to the hospital. She passed away on Christmas day. Needless to say the Christmas season would never be the same for the Culhane sisters and the restaurant staff. The loss of their dear friend would always stay with them. Apparently so has Barbara.

Spirited at the Pub

According to reports from the sisters themselves and the staff Barbara is still around the pub and the people she loved in spirit if not in body. Many of the staff have been encountering her ghost for the last several years. Especially Leeann, who was one of Barbara's best friends, and a member of Culhane's staff.

One of the encounters Leeann described involved the kitchen. The staff has always had a habit of putting the drink pitchers above the staff refrigerator. Barbara, while alive and managing the restaurant hated the pitchers being there and would always move

5

them to another location asking the staff as she did so to please, not put them up there. One day while Leeann was working she saw the pitchers come sailing off the top of the refrigerator, about three feet and land on the floor. There were no sudden wind gusts and no air handling vents close enough or powerful enough to hurl the pitchers from their position atop the staff refrigerator. This has happened more than once and the staff believe this is Barbara's way of saying she still doesn't want them there.

Barbara was also a very busy person, always going from one part of the pub to the other, making sure everything got done and the guests were happy. When she did so she had a very distinct walk that left a very unique sound as she passed. Many staff members have reported hearing Barbara's brisk walk hurrying by when they are preparing to open in the morning. Apparently Barbara is still on duty helping get the restaurant ready for the upcoming day.

My husband and I and several members of my Historic Haunts Investigations team often find ourselves enjoying a meal at Culhane's Irish Pub. We love the sisters and their food and when we heard about the activity at the pub, we were extremely interested. We are in the process of scheduling an investigation. Stay tuned to www.historic-haunts.net We will have information about the investigation on our blog page. In the meantime, this Irish pub known for its "Irish sass with four star class" seems to have one other spirit besides the ones behind the bar.

THE MYSTERIES OF BRADEN CASTLE
Braden Castle Ruins, Bradenton
••

In 1850 a Virginia native, Dr. Joseph Braden acquired 900 acres of land in an area of Florida near Sarasota. Upon that land he built a steam operated sugar and grist mill and a two story home with 20 inch thick tabby walls that stretched 100 feet high. Not the normal practice of the time, but prudent perhaps when your neighbors are unfriendly Indians. Dr. Braden's property would come to be known as Braden Plantation or perhaps more famously as Braden Castle.

Braden's History
In February of 1856 the Third Seminole War broke out. It was during this war that the "castle" was attacked at night by hostile Indians. Built for just such situations, Braden Castle proved a worthy encampment. Braden and house guests doused the downstairs lights and moved upstairs armed and ready for battle. They shot at the quickly moving shadows of their attackers and managed to drive them off. When the "battle" was over fourteen of Dr. Braden's slaves were gone (presumably dragged off into the woods) along with stolen blankets and mules. The doctor would lead an expedition the next day that would result in the deaths of several Indians and the retrieval of many of the taken items.

Despite his successful defense of the the Castle, 1857 saw Doctor Braden succumb not to Indians, but to financial debt as the Sugar Mill couldn't produce enough to meet the over $8,000 in notes owed at the time. Braden's main creditor Daniel Ladd fore-closed and Braden moved to Tallahassee (leaving his name as his only other legacy to the town). In 1867 Ladd sold the castle to a General and Mrs. Cooper. In 1876 General Cooper died and the house was abandoned.In 1903 a fire gutted most of the building leaving only the skeleton of the outer walls.

The castle was once again abandoned until 1924 when the committee of tourists bought the castle and grounds. Over the ensuing years they added men's and lady's clubs, built the Plaza park, a long pier and cottages. In the 1960s the castle began to deteriorate to ruins, In 1972, the state recognized the historic value of the ruins and in 1985 it was put on the National Register of Historic Places.

Reports of paranormal activity at the Castle
With incidents of violence with the Seminole Indians and slave labor used to build the castle, its no surprise that their might be some paranormal energy present. The Castle's proximity to the water and its limestone composition only add to the possibility of spir-its as both are thought to drain these types of energy. These conditions and the build-ing's history perhaps help justify why the ruins and surrounding area is thought by many witnesses to be haunted.

Strange noises have been reported at night coming from within the castle walls (despite the lack of people or situations to explain it). Others witness have reported pass-ing the building and hearing the sounds of heavy breathing behind them. When they turn

7

around to find the cause they discover no one else present. Police frequently investigate these reports only to find the empty remnants of an abandoned building.

If you visit the area, regardless of whether you experience anything supernatural or not, its an amazing place. The ruins and its outskirts have a haunting appearance that gives visitors some insight into Brandenton's historic past

THE ENERGIZED CASSADAGA HOTEL
Cassadaga Hotel, Cassadaga, Florida

The Amazing Cassadaga Hotel

A Deeply Spiritual Location

The Cassadaga Hotel has the elegance and traditional sophistication of a small intimate hotel from the 1920s. The hotel has been restored to preserve its original 1920s charm. Additional efforts have been made to allow guests to explore a variety of psychic and spiritual disciplines, whether in classrooms, in private sessions, in the wonderful gift shop, or even on a ghost tour.

Cassadaga Florida has been the center of spiritualist communities since 1894. There is reportedly an amazing vortex in the middle of Cassadaga near the hotel. Psychics and mediums feed off the energy in this town and claim it magnifies their abilities to a new level. Cassadaga is also known as the Psychic Center of the south. With all the energy still here in this little town it's no wonder the hotel is thought to house a few spirits.

Cassadaga's Resident Haunts

There are several spirits here at the hotel and one in particular is especially mischievous. He goes by the name of Gentleman Jack. He is a cigar smoking ladies' man and most often times shows himself when beautiful young woman are around. Some women have reported being whistled at and even being pinched on the buttocks.

There are also two little girl spirits named Sarah and Katlin who show up often and

9

who are very playful. People have reported hearing little girls giggling and running down the hallways. They also like to play with things and they never seem to put them back where they originally got them.

I talked with one woman who worked in the hotel when it was going through renovations. She and her adult daughter were hired to paint throughout the hotel. They were given permission to stay in the hotel while they painted so they could work any hour of the day or night.

During their first night they realized they had been painting all day and had gotten a lot of painting done. They were both exhausted from all the painting and retired to their rooms. They were the only two in the entire hotel. The woman I spoke with was startled in the middle of the night by loud noises in the hallway. She got up to see if her daughter had perhaps gotten up unable to sleep. As she got into the hallway she learned there was no one there and the noises had stopped. Immediately after the woman's daughter came out of her room to ask her mom what the noise was. There was no one to be found anywhere in the entire hotel.

The next day they both got up and started painting yet again and were talking about the noises they had heard the night before. They really couldn't even pin point what it sounded like but they both had heard it. The daughter claimed at one point in the night to have heard laughter and never did figure out where it was coming from. They both just kind of chalked it up to be an old building full of strange noises and went about their day.

As the day turned to evening and the sun started to set the atmosphere in the hotel started to change. An eerie feeling of heaviness started to emanate through the halls. The girls started to get a little creeped out, when suddenly a male apparition appeared in the hallway watching them. He literally materialized in front of them and he did not feel like a friendly presence.

The ladies ran to their rooms, grabbed their personal stuff, and got the heck out of there. When they got out of the hotel and started discussing what they both had just experienced, they both agreed whoever it was it didn't want them there. Maybe the ghost didn't like the choices of paint colors.

Sometimes renovations on a building can stir up spirits from the past. Sometimes the spirits are trying to figure out what is going on in "their" buildings, often times they don't understand the changes that are being made, then others like that someone is caring for "their" space and want to show the people they appreciate what is going on there.

The next day the two ladies called the manager of the Cassadaga Hotel and explained what had happened and why the painting stuff wasn't put away. The manager told the women that the spirit they saw was Arthur and he probably didn't like the renovations going on in "his" building. He has never harmed anyone but he has scared quite a few.

The two decided they would finish the job, but from that point on they would be finished and out of the building before dusk set in. The next day when they went in to paint they told the ghost they weren't there to hurt him they were just there to try and make the place look nice. They didn't see anything after that but they did make sure to be out of there before night fall.

To this day Cassadaga still seems to enjoy the company of its resident haunts. The

10

two little girls still seem to be there playing in the hotel and moving things around on people and laughing and giggling in the halls. Apparently Jack is still there, and very happy to say hello to the pretty ladies. Even Arthur still shows up from time to time.

Historic Haunts Investigates the Cassadaga

I was fortunate enough to investigate here in September 2012 and had a few personal experiences myself. I also learned there are a few other haunts here besides the ones previously mentioned.

During the investigation I experienced a little boy and girl named Diane and Steven. They were actually staying in the room I had reserved for the night. Room #25 and #26 are actually two attached rooms at the hotel with a bathroom in the middle. Two of my investigators traveled with me and they slept in room #25 which had two beds, while I slept in room #26 that had one. The room that they occupied is where the children like to play in the closet. The room I was in had a gentleman that reportedly liked to crawl into bed, whether you were in it or not. I didn't experience the gentleman, but I did hear giggling and footsteps in the night which I believe were the children.

Cassadaga also experiences the apparition of a woman who is seen walking the hallway. Not a lot is known about her, but she has been physically seen on multiple occasions. She is seen in a long flowing dress and her hair is set atop her head in a style that seems to be from the 1920s. Many think she is an originally owner or guest of the hotel. I didn't encounter this woman's spirit, but I did get responses on my equipment in the classrooms and several other rooms at the hotel.

While in the class room area we had major activity from the REM Pod and the Mel Meter Hybrid. The meters were both going off in the one corner of the room and there were absolutely no electrical sources to explain the activity. We asked the spirits yes or no question and they would respond to the questions.

Like the classroom area, Room #24 had major K2 EMF Meter activity and we were able to get questions answered with flashlights in this area as well.

The Cassadaga Hotel is an unusual and unique location. There seems to be a lot of spiritual energy in play at the hotel and in the town in general. For fans of the paranormal Cassadaga Hotel is a very active place where you are almost guaranteed to have a paranormal experience, but I didn't run into anything malevolent. Maybe the ladies who were helping with the renovations just weren't used to the spirit world and it really got to them?

THE HAUNTS OF THE FORMER FORT HARRISON HOTEL

Former Fort Harrison Hotel, Clearwater

••

The former Fort Harrison Hotel is the flagship building of Flag Land Base, the Church of Scientology's spiritual headquarters in Clearwater. The building has seen much in its time. While it currently provides an area for visiting Scientology practitioners to be housed, fed and trained, it once housed the spring training Philadelphia Phillies, jazz legends Count Basie and Duke Ellington, and the Rolling Stones while they wrote their hit "(I Can't Get No) Satisfaction" there at the hotel (1965). Unfortunately, visitors to the hotel on weekdays won't get any satisfaction either being denied access unless they belong to the church. Die hard fans can visit the L. Ron Hubbard exhibit or the hotel's restaurant during the hotel's tour day on Sundays. While paranormal fans may not be able to get inside during the week, they can still read of its background and perhaps gain insight into the unusual phenomenon that continues there to this day.

The History of the Fort Harrison

Clearwater in the 1920's was a booming Florida town. So much so that "snowbirds" and visitors taking in the city's healthful climate and picturesque surroundings often swamped the city's small hotels. Recognizing the need for a large luxury hotel, Clearwater city planners turned to real estate broker and developer Ed Haley. He quickly procured the land and the funds and construction began in 1925. On December 31st, 1926 a gala celebration and grand opening were held to welcome the new building and the new year. Guests from all over including Pinellas County were treated to the comforts and conveniences the hotel offered and caused some to refer to the Fort Harrison as the aristocrat among Florida hotels. Ransom E. Olds, inventor of the Oldsmobile operated the hotel from 1926 until his death in 1950.

The Fort Harrison would continue to service the community with its lavish accommodations, events and activities. Though these activities decreased significantly during the Great Depression, the hotel still did its part to provide a symbol of pride for the Clearwater community.

During the war time era of the 1940's the hotel housed U.S. Army and Air Force personnel and benefits for the American Red Cross. The majority of the military personnel had left by the summer of 1943, and The Fort Harrison returned to the business of being a luxury hotel.

The 1950's saw Clearwater experiencing the same post-war boom the rest of the country enjoyed. Highways into town were widened and bridges into town were added. In 1953, the hotel was purchased by the Jack Tar Corporation. The years that followed saw extensive renovations that brought the hotel cabanas, air conditioning in all rooms, an expanded mezzanine, a 1500 seat auditorium, and 85 new guest rooms.

By 1963 the hotel had been renovated again and had joined the automation age. A closed-circuit tv registration system allowed guests to drive into the Auto Lobby

12

where they could receive their room keys by pneumatic tube. In its efforts to provide a major and thoroughly modern convention center, a lounge with super club, and Japanese gardens for holding special events were added.

The 1970's brought new development and other draws and theme parks that pulled people away from central Clearwater. The hotel itself was experiencing a jazz renaissance with big head-liners performing concerts including Count Basie, Duke Ellington, and Buddy Rich. Unfortunately, even this was not enough to halt the declining hotel business, its owners decided to sell and in 1975 this eleven story, two-hundred and twenty room marvel was purchased by the Church of Scientology under the name of "Southern Land Development and Leasing Corp." and "United Churches of Florida Inc." The church wished to turn Fort Harrison into the center of its new international religious retreat.

In 1976, it went through a $2.8 million restoration project. The former Fort Harrison Hotel saw further detailed renovations in 1985. Under the stewardship of the church former efforts to "modernize" were restored to their original luster. In 2007 the church announced another $20 million restoration project would take place next, but not when it would start.

Unusual Occurrences at the Former Hotel

Since 1975 there have been at least three mysterious deaths in the building. Lisa McPherson died in the building on December 5th of 1995 after spending 17 days in room #174. In February 1980, Scientologist Joseph A. Havenith was found dead in his bath tub. The water in the bath was hot enough to have burned his skin off, but the officially reported cause of death was drowning. This despite the fact, that the coroner claimed that when he was found his head was not submerged.

In August 1988, Heribert Pfaff died of a seizure after not taking his medicine in favor of his recently replaced vitamin program. In 1997 the Clearwater Police Department received over 160 emergency calls from the building, but upon arrival were denied entry by the Scientology security. With the hotel's past and the unusual events that have occurred over the last thirty years, it isn't a stretch to believe its haunted. There are numerous reports of paranormal activity from outside the hotel by non church members.

Fort Harrison's paranormal

Some reports describe seeing transparent faces looking out the top windows of the building, many of these often appear in photos. Other witnesses have reported capturing a strange misty fog in photos on certain clear nights.

While I personally have no knowledge of exactly what has gone on in the church over the last thirty-nine years, driving by this building ever since I was a little kid has always creeped me out. Now that I have learned more of the buildings history and paranormal accounts, there is definitely something unsettling about this once grand hotel icon. Perhaps the future will shed more light on this Clearwater Historic Haunt.

THE GHOST OF HARDEN HOUSE
Harden House, Clermont
....

Murdered in Cold Blood

John Harden woke up in the middle of the night in 1975 to find his truck in a blaze in his yard. As he ran outside to see what was going on, he was killed by a shot gun at close range. The murderer escaped and has never been captured. The story appeared on a variety of news outlets and even found its way to the popular "Unsolved Mysteries" series. Even with all the press, the authorities were still unable to apprehend the killer.

Sometime after the killing, a woman by the name of June Farris began having nightmares of a house that she had never seen before. She had the same dream over and over again and in incredibly distinct detail. Repeatedly in her dreams, she saw herself running down a back staircase in the house and out the back door. This dream made absolutely no sense to her but she always woke up scared or in a panic from what she saw.

A few years passed and her family bought an old house in Clermont and Once they began to move in she quickly realized this was the house from her dream.

Occupying Spirits

Strange things started to happen shortly after June and her family moved into the house. An apparition of a man appeared frequently and heavy footsteps were often heard. June learned more about Harden's murder and was shocked to discover that the night he was killed he had run down the back stairs and out the back door. She started to think that it was Harden who was haunting the house and seeking justice. The hauntings and paranormal activity continued and increased over time

Eventually, June and her family sold the house to this day the the murder has never been solved. New owners have since bought the house. The new owners are die-hard non believers in ghosts. When asked about a paranormal presence in the house the new owners claimed that he felt "vibrations" of peace and if there were any ghosts, the good ones ran off the bad ones. He lived there for 20 years and never experienced a thing.

Maybe the spirit has moved on, or maybe he is just seeking the right person to help him put an end to his unsolved death. There is evidence to support the fact that paranormal entities to some degree avoid disbelievers preferring instead to manifest to those people open to listening to them.

John Harden it seems, might still be looking for someone to listen to him.

YEAR ROUND SPIRITS AT THE AUGUST SEVEN
August Seven Inn, Daytona Beach

The beautiful August Seven Inn

This house is clean, or at least you'd think it would be considering who built it. James N. Gamble of Proctor and Gamble cleaning products fame built a guest house in 1896 across the street from his inter-coastal mansion. His home unfortunately, burned down long ago, but the guest house lived on and is now the August Seven Inn.

This quaint inn with its Victorian architecture and modern amenities has been carefully and lovingly restored and listed on the National Historic Register. It is known for being a Certificate of Excellence winner and recognized as one of the "select few small inns of Daytona Beach". To fans of the paranormal, however, it has yet another distinction, it's haunted!

Historic Haunts Investigations had the opportunity to investigate the Inn in May 2014. We were initially drawn to her by the reputation of the Inn and the interesting stories about the paranormal that had reached us.

Joseph Dirsa, the owner, filled us in on some of the history and the antiques within. He also shared some of his and his guests' ghostly encounters.

Tales of the August Seven

One morning when Joe was beginning to open up the front room for the day he glanced into the sitting room and saw a woman on the couch. He opened the French doors to the spa room and turned around to greet the woman and somehow in that

15

split second she had vanished. Other guests have encountered this spectral woman and have reported remarkably similar incidents, her exact identity is unknown.

Besides paranormal incidents involving the mystery woman, guests and employees at the inn have felt like they were being followed when ascending the stairs to go to their rooms. Almost as if someone was behind them practically breathing down their necks. When these guests or employees turn around to see who is on the steps with them, they find no one. Joan, Joe's mother even had her own encounter to share. It occurred in the basement near the laundry room. She felt a breath on her neck, she thought it was Joe and when she turned around she realized she was completely alone. There were no air vents or fans to provide an obvious reason for the sudden burst of air.

Other reports at the Inn describe the phantom scents of "old-timey" perfume or food being cooked. Employees and guests search for the phantom smells but can never discover where they are coming from. Once again many of these scents spring up in rooms away from kitchen cooking, scented bathroom/hygiene products in restrooms, or other obvious explanations.

One guest who stayed in the carriage house wrote in the room guest book that she was awoken in the middle of the night by the apparition of a man standing by the bed looking at her. When she woke her husband up, he too saw the same ghostly image, before the the man vanished. This type of activity was among the most commonly reported in the Carriage House and a great example of why we were excited to come investigate.

The Team Investigates

Sometimes, many times actually, we do an investigation that ends up fairly uneventful. As I often like to say ghosts and spirits (like living people) don't necessarily perform on command. However, we did encounter one particularly unusual thing that night during our investigation and that was in room 1022. It was in this room, thought to be haunted, that the K2 EMF meter kept going off like crazy with high EMFs on the right side of the bed. When we moved the meter away it would go back to normal. We examined the room closely (especially the right side of the bed), but we couldn't find any electrical, sub-flooring electrical,temperature or other electric components that could explain the K2 readings.

The Post Investigation

Not only do spirits or entities typically avoid manifesting on cue, they sometimes seem to enjoy waiting until the cameras and recording devices stop before making themselves known. This was the case at the Inn after the formal investigation was complete. Team members Gayel and Jim Roush were along on this investigation and they stayed in room 1022 while I was in room 819. We didn't learn until later that we both had the same thing happen to each of us at exactly 2:30 a.m.

I had been woken up from a sound sleep by a hot rod car out on the main road and was trying to nod back off when I heard the door knob slightly jiggle, followed by clearly audible footsteps leading up to the widow's walk, but there was no living person outside the door or in the area. The next morning as I arrived for breakfast, the first of my team, I shared this experience with Phillip one of the staff members at the inn before any other members of my team arrived. A short time later, after breakfast Gayel shared a story of her own with Joe Dirsa and myself. This story was very familiar as she described the exact same incident I had encountered the night before right down to the loud vehicle waking her, the jiggling door nob, and the time. We were shocked because neither one of us had told the other about it until then. Upon further consideration we concluded that it was highly unlikely to have been a living person walking up to the widow's peak because the area is now used as storage. It is also almost completely packed with little to no space between objects in the room. It would have been virtually impossible for someone to walk up there and not bang into anything, especially in the dark.

Unfortunately, in the case of many investigations some of the most unusual or compelling incidents occur when everything is packed up or in the process. This was decidedly the case with the August Seven Inn. Still, the spirits here at the inn are harmless and the staff is amazing and we wanted to thank Joe and his staff for a memorable stay and investigation. We also recommend this Inn to those traveling to Daytona Beach, whether into the paranormal or not. It's a great destination with wonderful rooms and amenities at one of America's most scenic and enjoyable beaches.

17

THE SPIRITS OF THE PLAZA
The Plaza Resort & Spa, Daytona Florida

The Plaza Resort & Spa street side

During the summer months the beach is where many people want to be! This is still the case today and was certainly the case in the later part of the 1800s. Boats and the railroad made Daytona and Florida beaches a popular tourist destination for the wealthy (Daytona Beach was actually the "end of the line" for Henry Flagler's Railroad). Thus it was no surprise that an enterprising man by the name of Charles Ballough decided to upgrade his large beach cottage at the end of Ocean Boulevard to accommodate the influx of visitors. This expanded cottage would be named "The Clarendon" and would be the first incarnation of what would eventually become the Plaza Resort.

Not long after The Clarendon opened Charles Ballough formed a partnership with another local businessman. The result of his partnership was the combining of several properties including The Clarendon, The Breakers (on the north side), and a 1,200 foot pier (on the south). The joined properties were dubbed "The Clarendon Hotel". They boasted features like casinos, spacious porches overlooking the ocean, and stable/livery for horses and carriages. It was no surprise that The Clarendon Hotel would become enormously successful.

An Unexpected Tragedy

At the height of the Clarendon's popular winter season in February of 1909 a fire broke out. The hotel was full of "snow birds" guests from up north visiting Florida to escape the cold northern winters. These same guests were rushed out of The

18

Clarendon and put up at a nearby hotel as the entire hotel was engulfed in flames and destroyed. Many stayed on the beach for hours watching in disbelief as the grand hotel burned. The fire, thought to have started in the kitchen, devastated the entire hotel.

Rising from the Ashes

By May 1909, three months later, a group of Philadelphia architects completed plans for a brand new "fire proof" Clarendon and on New Year's Day in 1911 the new seven story Clarendon, opened its doors. Guests would soon discover the grandeur of the "new" hotel as they encountered rooms built of solid mahogany, with glass door knobs, and marble floors. These guests would also be treated to luxurious Turkish baths, trap shooting, horseback riding, and an 18 hole golf course.

The Hotel's Love Affair with Flight

Just one month into its new opening, Daytona City leaders and The Clarendon would embark on an amazing promotion that would distinguish the hotel for many years to come. The successful maiden voyage of the Wright Brothers flight had only happened eight years prior. The novelty of manned flight still remained a popular curiosity of the time. The Clarendon and the city of Daytona would capitalize on this by bringing John A.D. McCurdy's "Silver Dart" airplane, by train, to Daytona. Visitors and residents would be treated to a series of three flights along the beach, but there would be much more to come.

Preferred parking for planes photo courtesy of The Plaza Resort & Spa

By 1912, arrangements were made for some guests from the north during the winter to be flown in by pilot and plane. A landing strip just south of the hotel and hanger were constructed by The Clarendon for these guests. The innovation was nothing new to The Clarendon, so it was no great surprise that one of the hotel's pilots, Ruth Law, would become the first woman to "loop" an airplane, a feat she accomplished in front of the hotel in 1915. By the time WWI came about it was fairly common to see the beach in front of the hotel littered with parked airplanes. Many of these were pilots on their way to training in Jacksonville who needed a place to stop and rest after a long flight. After the war ended the tradition continued as 1920 even found the Wrigley Flying Circus landing their planes in front of the hotel. Unfortunately, it wasn't too long after this that increased visitation to the beach and the hotel by people and automobiles made beach landings by aviators dangerous and impractical.

Becoming the Plaza

Just before the great depression hit the hotel came under the Harrington Mills. It struggled on valiantly through this hard economic time until the U.S. entered World War II. From 1942-1944 the hotel closed for the war effort and served as barracks for the Women's Army Corps.

In June of 1944 the hotel was reopened and renamed the Sheraton Plaza. Sheraton would go on to sell the property for $1 million dollars and it would be renamed again, this time as The Craig Hotel.

In 1957 the hotel made world news when word got out that Col. Rudolf Abel, a Russian spy, had stayed at the hotel. Life Magazine even ran pictures of the hotel, unwanted publicity when the Cold War was heating up.

In March of 1963 this forward thinking hotel would again take risks hoping to cash in on Daytona Beach's convention industry. The Craig Hotel underwent the first of many renovations to restore the old hotel's "grandeur" under owners Jacob Fine and Milton Pepper. Unfortunately, despite Daytona's popularity as a spring break destination the convention industry didn't explore as anticipated. In 1974, the bank foreclosed on owner Jacob Fine. The bank sold off the hotels furnishings and the top floors were removed. Much later in 1998 the hotel was purchased by Charles Bray and Joe Gillespie and they reopened it as the Ocean Waters Spa in 2000.

The hurricane season of 2004 hit hard and the hotel was ravaged by three hurricanes. The Plaza Resort and Spa (as it is named today) stands strong and has been exquisitely restored. Still, it seems the Plaza does have a few secrets. Though long dead, a few people from the hotel's past have apparently never left.

The History of the Paranormal at the Plaza

Besides its turbulent past and natural disasters, the hotel has seen a lot of deaths (and violent ones at that). In 2012 alone, there were an estimated 8 deaths at the Plaza; among them a hanging, a window jumper, and a decapitation to name a few. Its no wonder then that there are many reports of paranormal activity at The Plaza.

One of the most common involves a man in overalls who is believed to have been a maintenance man. His spirit is often seen in the Grande Colonnade. Though often appearing as an appari-

The Grande Colonnade Area
photo courtesy of the Plaza Resort & Spa

tion he has also been described as a shadow figure seen frequently by guests and staff in the area.

Plaza (building) A has endured a multitude of reports over the years describing childish giggling and the sound of a ball bouncing, mainly on the 14th floor. The 14th floor (which is actually the 13th) but has been renumbered for superstitious reasons like many other hotel,has frequent childlike activity. The apparitions of a 7 year old little girl named Penelope and a little boy named Orville are often seen in and around Room #1409.

Besides the 14th floor, the 11th floor has witnessed a lot of paranormal activity. In fact, rooms #1111 and #1112 are reported to be very active as well. Witnesses have described experiencing everything from cold spots to voices in the bathrooms and these are just a couple of the paranormal occurrences reported there. Further, it seems whatever entity may be in Room #1112, it doesn't seem to want to interact with female guests.

While many paranormal incidents occur in the rooms and open guest areas, the staff report frequent activity in areas typically reserved for hotel employees. The kitchen area for example, has been described as having a very heavy feeling throughout. Many seem to believe this could be possibly due to the fire in the kitchen which burned down the original hotel. Remnants of the old kitchen can still be found at the Plaza. Its in these areas that hotel employees describe lights which frequently flicker or turn on and off on their own accord. Though the electrical wiring in this area has been checked frequently there has been no plausible reason for this activity. It has been suggested that some of the employees who died in the 1909 might still be here and wanting attention.

In addition to the kitchen, the basement has frequent paranormal activity as well. The elevator has a tendency to go to the basement of its own accord and the doors will open as if letting someone out. This happens even when no one has been in the elevator or pushed any buttons, this occurs at all hours of the day and night, even when the guests are asleep. Employees have also described items in the basement being moved or "disappearing" only to "reappear" later.

Our First Investigation

Historic Haunts Investigations had the opportunity to investigate here in November 2013 and we had a few experiences of our own.

In an effort to be thorough we began our investigation as we usually do by chatting with several members of the amazing staff at the resort. They shared many of their encounters and those of several guests. It would seem that Paranormal activity seems to occur at The Plaza almost daily. Craig Lew, one of the hotel's security guards has encountered a variety of paranormal activity at The Plaza, but told us the only place in the entire hotel that "creeps him out" is room #1111, the room we were (coincidentally staying in). As we later learned from him and other employees there are many reports of guests feeling nauseous suddenly after a short time in the room and having a strong, but inexplicable desire to want to get a different room. One guest described an incident in which he claimed someone unseen, a voice in the room told him to jump off the balcony, but there was certainly no one else in the room. This guest was so frightened he went straight to the front desk and asked for a security guard to walk him to his car, he was leaving. After doing some digging we discovered that several years ago, a man checked in to Room #1111 and committed suicide by jumping from the balcony.

We investigated our haunted room thoroughly and we were surprised to encounter A LOT of K2 activity. We did a base reading of the room and of the electrical items in the room, but none of them were putting off any significant EMF. The EMF readings we did repeatedly get were in the dead center of the room or centered on the 2 chairs near the balcony. We investigated the possibility of hidden wiring in these areas but found none and were told by hotel staff there were no electrical sources running through these areas.

We moved on from our room to investigate the haunts of the 14th floor. We were told by staff that a young spirit by the name of Penelope, a little girl known to have died in the fire, likes to mess with some of the staff and the guests. She has even followed security guard Craig Lew home! Wilson, another hotel staff member has experienced Penelope as well. She tugged on his pant legs one night trying to get his attention. Many, including the staff have heard a little girl giggle in the colonnade area of the hotel and in some of the ballrooms while the area was vacant. Some suggest this might be Penelope. If so it is the perfect place for a little girl to play.

While we were doing interviews in the colonnade area, with Craig, Wilson and others we were repeatedly getting spikes on the K2 meter all at about waist level, maybe it was Penelope, and it was about her height.

We moved on to investigate other areas of the hotel. We encountered a few unusual EMF readings in the area where the original kitchen had existed before it had burned. With no distinct entities to blame for this activity and with the fluctuating EMF readings we considered that this could just be residual energy from the people who died in the fire that destroyed much of the hotel.

There are many other spirits at the hotel mentioned, but that we unfortunately didn't encounter on this visit. Like the boy Oliver and the maintenance man. Though they are often seen or encountered in different parts of the hotel, we never came across them. As active as the hotel was during our initial investigation, we knew we wanted to return to investigate again, and the hotel graciously agreed.

Historic Haunts Returns

During our second investigation we stayed in Room #1409 in hopes of running into Penelope. Curiously, just a few nights before a guest had reported to the staff an apparition of the little girl. Unfortunately, we didn't experience anything, and in fact, we encountered little to no activity throughout the hotel. However, I realized something after the fact. We had gone out earlier in the day to another Daytona location to investigate and because this location was thought to have a more dangerous entity haunting it, I was wearing my protection crystal. I completely forgot to take it off before the Plaza investigation.

Some crystals are thought by some to deter spirits, good or bad. It also goes to show that even seasoned paranormal investigators sometimes make-absent minded mistakes. There is one thing I learned a long time ago, when doing an investigation if you are WANTING to experience something, don't wear any protection medals, crosses, or crystals.

Our Thoughts on the Plaza

The Plaza is an amazing place and we hope to investigate there again. Whether you experience the paranormal here at the hotel or not; it is a must see while in Daytona, but there are several in this town (check out the Ponce Inlet Lighthouse which was featured in my first book, Historic Haunts Florida).

Recommendation

Do you want to investigate the Plaza Resort and Spa, but are too scared to do it on your own? Contact www.americanghostadventures.com and sign up for one of the paranormal events at this haunted Daytona hot spot. American Ghost Adventures is one of the most experienced paranormal group you can investigate with that conducts public investigations. They frequently investigate the Plaza and often encounter unusual evidence themselves.

THE WAILING STARKEY
AT THE BLUE ANCHOR
The Blue Anchor Pub & Restaurant, Delray Beach

Sometimes there are haunted locations whose backgrounds seem to be tied to objects. The spirits there are almost tethered to a particular thing. One of the more interesting of these is the Blue Anchor in Delray Beach.

Ties to London

It is said that in 1888 two of Jack the Ripper's victims (Elizabeth Stride and Catherine Eddows) were both seen drinking at The Blue Anchor with well-to-do gentlemen the night they were murdered. The building was originally constructed by William Younger Brewery (Hence the "Wm Younger" proudly displayed above the front door). Winston Churchill even reportedly walked through those original wooden doors.

Built originally in 1864, on the site of a 17th century coaching inn, the pub welcomed many famous faces in its well over 100 years of existence before it was taken down for a parking lot.

The Blue Anchor Comes to America

What does this old London pub have to do with Delray Beaches Blue Anchor you ask? Well, in 1996 many of the pieces of that old London pub were sent over the Atlantic on a ship and reconstruction of the pub began. Original oak panels, doors, stained glass windows, and even the eight foot tall English Oak front doors were all installed in the new pub. Visitors to the newest incarnation of the pub are greeted by signs welcoming them "Back to foggy London Town and to the days when Jack the Ripper prowled the shadowy streets and Queen Victoria ruled the free world."

The Haunted Blue Anchor

For well over 100 years, the building (at its old and new locations) has been haunted by a young woman named Bertha Starkey. Starkey was reportedly stabbed to death in the original London pub by her jealous seafaring husband after he found out that she had been having an affair.

Light footsteps attributed to a woman and chilling wails are often heard from the bar late at night. One year, on the anniversary of her death, a thick glass shelf was even observed to shatter for no apparent reason. Candles have also been known to put themselves out, and then relight a few moments later. Attempts to debunk or recreate some of these paranormal phenomenon have been unsuccessful. The Blue Anchor apparently still holds some supernatural secrets.

I recommend a visit if you are in the area. This is truly a great piece of American and English history and is a hauntingly charming place to enjoy "spirits with spirits".

24

RUINS AND INDIANS AND CRYPTIDS ...OH MY!

Bulow Plantation Ruins, Flagler Beach

Bulow Plantation Ruins

In 1821 Major Charles Wilhelm Bulow used slave labor to clear 2200 acres and planted sugar cane, cotton, rice, and indigo in an area that is now considered Flagler Beach. Soon after Charles' death, his son John took over the planation and it prospered for many years. During its peak the Bulow Plantation covered 4,675 acres, but now consists of 150 acres with the ruins still standing. The plantation thrived until the Second Seminole War.

Braving Indian Attacks and Illness

In 1836, the Seminole Indians burned "Bulowville" along with several other plantations in the area. Bulow was thought to be a big supporter of the Seminole tribe and he tried to keep Major Benjamin Putnam away from his property and from the Indians. It is said that in 1835 he was taken prisoner and the Raiders used his plantation as an outpost to wage war on the tribe.

The war with the Seminole Indians was suddenly less important when yellow fever broke out and Putnam and his men released Bulow and fled back to St. Augustine. Unfortunately, by this time the Seminole tribe thought Bulow had sided with the military and betrayed them. That's when they burned the plantation. Shortly after the burning of the plantation and with little else to stay for Bulow left for Paris. His Paris retreat would be short, as he died only 3 months later at the age of 26.

25

Local Myths and Legends

Many locals believe the Seminole Indians cursed the men with yellow fever and cursed the land as well. There are many different reports of unusual and paranormal activity in the area. They vary from the subjective paranormal sciences to cryptozoology. For starters many guests to the area report seeing strange balls of light in the woods. If these reports are not enough to catch a paranormal fan's interests there are also numerous reports of cold spots felt throughout the area, even on the hottest of days. Still other reports describe the appearance of shadow figures around the ruins and the sensation by many witnesses that they are being watched. Curious, when the woods are known to be devoid of people.

In addition, there are multiple reports of an alleged "cryptid" creature said to be lurking in the woods and the swampy area surrounding the property. Most of these reports describe a swamp monster that moved at great speed and disturbs the trees as he runs through them. It has been suggested that perhaps it is trying to run people out of his territory.

Our experiences at Bulow

Coincidentally during our visit, the day we were here researching the property and taking photos of the ruins I saw something very large with brownish red hair dart quickly through the woods. At the time my husband was exploring another part of the property. I caught up with him and described what I saw. We began an intense search for an animal or some other explanation, but we never found a thing. It moved so fast I couldn't provide any other details. I didn't even know there were reported incidents of the existence of a cryptid creature until returning home and reading about it later.

Regardless of whether you believe in swamp monsters or ghosts, the Bulow Plantation ruins are some of the most beautiful ruins I've seen in the sunshine state. They are easily well worth a side trip for history and paranormal fans alike. If you go be sure to bring a camera and keep an eye out for great photo opportunities and your ears open for rustling in the woods.

Bulow Plantation Ruins and the forest surrounding it.

THE ENAMORED ENTITY OF CORAL CASTLE

Coral Castle, Homestead

A Tragic Love Story

Situated in lower Florida, near Homestead is an amazing testament to one man's dedication and love. This iconic local landmark has been drawing tourists since the 1940's. It remains one of the most unusual structures in the state, and is known as the Coral Castle. The Coral Castle is a love story contained in coral, but wouldn't have come about without the hard work and dedication of Edward Leeds Kalnin. Kalnin was born in Riga Latvia in 1887. At the age of 26 he was engaged to marry his one true love, 16 year old named Agnes Scuffs. He called her "Sweet Sixteen" and was truly in love with his bride to be. To his everlasting dismay, she canceled the wedding one day before the ceremony was to take place. Kalnin was devastated.

A Testament in Coral

He moved to Florida City in 1918 seeking a better climate to help cure his tuberculosis. and his still broken heart. It was shortly after this that Kalnin began to consider an outlet for the dedication he felt to the woman he never got over. However, he wouldn't begin his monumental efforts until 1936 when he moved to Homestead. It was there that he would start one of the most unusual projects in the state and a testament to for his devotion to Agnes.

Despite being a smaller man at just five feet tall and around one hundred pounds, and owning only a bicycle for transportation, Kalnin would virtually single-handedly build and sculpt a castle out of eleven hundred tons of coral rock (he did get a little help moving the larger pieces onto his property from a friend who owned a tractor). He then started a lifelong quest to create a monument to his beloved. He single handedly built Coral Castle, carving and sculpting 1100 tons of coral rock. Many wonder how he did this all on his own. He barely weighed 100 pounds himself and was just at 5 feet tall. He cut and moved these large pieces or coral stone all on his own.

It took Edward three years, beginning in 1936 when he moved to Homestead, to build his monument to Agnes. He did have a little help from a friend who owned a tractor which he used for moving the large pieces onto his property. Edward never learned to drive but he did ride a bicycle, but that wouldn't help me the large stones.

Each section is 8 feet tall and 4 feet wide and 3 feet thick. It took Kalnin the better part of three years to complete his monument to Agnes. The castle was constructed of multiple sections each eight feet tall, four feet wide, and three feet thick, all carved lovingly and ornately finished. By 1940, everything was perfectly completed and in place, word of his castle had spread and people were dying to see the finished project and testament to true love that this man created. They came from all around to tour Coral Castle. Entrance fees varied between ten cents and twenty-five cents depending on the tour.

In December 1951, Kalnin became very sick and put a note on the castle saying "Going to the hospital". He took the bus to Jackson Memorial Hospital in Miami where he died three days later in his sleep at age of 64.

27

His nephew, who lived in Michigan, inherited the castle and in 1953 while going through his uncle's things, came across 35 $100 bills that Edward had stashed away which was his life savings and total collected from his castle tours.

Today, Coral Castle has guests visiting from all over the world. Many come to see a love sick man's beautiful work of art inspired by his soul mate. Though Edward Kalnin died in 1951, many believe his spirit never left. There have been many reports describing Ed's apparition walking throughout the castle.

The Strange Phenomenon of the Castle

Besides reports and evidence of Kalnin's ghost captured visually by some and recorded by others the castle has several other unusual properties. It has been suggested that this may have been caused by the once living coral used to construct the castle or something about the site that drew Kalnin to it to begin with. Many people have reported an energy vortex within the castle walls. It has been described in detail even by people who have never even heard of a vortex. Vortexes are unusual concentrations of spinning or unseen energies. They can be felt by those within and are often the cause of sudden and unexpected ailments or illnesses, including fatigue, vertigo, headaches, stress, and others. In extreme cases these phenomenon are reported to even lift, move, or damage unfortunate people caught in their path. Guests to Coral Castle often describe to employees at the attraction what they've felt, and are told what they experienced wasn't their imagination or merely vertigo.

Whether you go to Coral Castle seeking the lovesick ghost or to view an unusual Florida attraction. Its detail and purpose make it worth seeing, even if it wasn't haunted. If you are a true fan of Florida's Historic Haunts its definitely one to add to your to do list.

PARANORMAL AUDIENCE PARTICIPATION
Florida Theatre, Jacksonville

The Florida Theatre marquee

Who doesn't enjoy a fun night out at the theatre? People have enjoyed catching shows at theatres since the time of Shakespeare. While there are many amazing historic theatres in the U.S. few can match the beautiful Florida Theatre in Jacksonville.

The Theatre's History

The Florida Theatre of Jacksonville is an example of beautiful Mediterranean Revival architecture. The theatre opened April 8th, 1927. It was designed by Roy Benjamin with the interior design done by R.E. Hall from New York. The interior design was an attempt to capture the look of a Moorish courtyard at night,complete with a star filled sky surrounded by fountains and balconies. The building itself originally also had a roof top garden.

The theatre hosted stage shows, motion pictures,stage shows, motion pictures, comedy shorts, and many other events. Unlike other theatres it even survived the great depression. In 1956, Elvis Presley came to Jacksonville and specifically the Florida Theatre for one of his first headline concert appearances on an indoor stage. The result was a Life Magazine feature story about Elvis' appearance at the Florida Theatre. Juvenile Court Judge, Marion Gooding sat through the entire show to make sure Elvis didn't get too provocative with his moves. Elvis was clever and stood behind the piano while he performed to hide his gyrating moves.

Unfortunately over time, despite locally produced opera, dance, and drama now being presented at the theatre, attendance went gradually downhill and the theatre closed on May 8th, 1980. In 1981 grants from the state of Florida and the City of Jacksonville, along with substantial private sector commitments, helped the Arts Assembly of Jacksonville (now the Cultural Council) save the theatre.

In 1987, the theatre separated from the Assembly and became its own independent entity after going through a $4.1 million restoration project. The glorious theatre now hosts about 200 events a year.

29

The Theatre's Haunts

There have been such a wide variety of events held here that one would think any paranormal activity in the place would be tied to the stage or a specific production. The Florida Theatre is haunted but not due to someone being murdered or falling to their death as some people have reported. Instead it seems that a guest who just really enjoyed the theatre in life doesn't want to leave.

An apparition was caught on camera sitting in the balcony at seat E2 section 500 by a local paranormal show. It was later featured on a nationwide paranormal show that tried to debunk the video. They were unable to accurately debunk it and in fact during the filming of their nationwide show, they also picked up heat signatures throughout the theatre. Cold spots are felt in different areas of the theatre, humming sounds have been heard, and several EVPs have been captured. Besides the resident spirit seated in the audience, theatre goers and staff have reported other unusually incidents.

We Check it Out for Ourselves

We had the opportunity to tour the entire theatre in the hopes of encountering some phenomenon ourselves or meeting one of the resident ghosts. Unfortunately we only had a few experiences while here. One of these occurred while I was in one of the dressing rooms. As soon as I entered the room, I was hit by a wave of Vertigo as soon as I stepped in! As soon as I left the room, I felt fine. We couldn't leave the theatre without checking out the infamous seat for ourselves and sure enough, we also got some strange EMF readings off the haunted seat in the upper level of the theatre. While the electrical wiring of the theatre easily explains high EMF and equipment fluctuations in other parts of the theatre, there were no such items to explain the readings from the seat in question.

If you want a great historic tour of the Florida Theatre you can do so, check their website for times and dates at certain times of the month the tour is free. However, this tour is definitely concentrated on the history of the building so don't go in thinking it is a ghost tour, because it won't be.

If you don't want the historical tour you can also go to movies, concerts, and other events at this grand theatre and experience the incredible acoustics, and near perfect sight lines in one of the 1,900 seats.

To me the Florida Theatre is a wonderfully restored example of what the high-style movie "palaces" used to look like and an amazing Historic Haunt.

Rear View of The Florida Theatre with painted advertisement

THE SPIRITED BEACHES MUSEUM & HISTORY CENTER

Beaches Museum & History Center, Jacksonville Beach

The Beaches Museum & History Center

While doing research in 2011 for my first book, Historic Haunts Florida, at The Beaches Museum and History Center, I learned the museum was haunted. With other stories taking up my research time, I didn't include it in the book, but kept the story in the back of my mind and vowed to return to it later.

Keeping My Promise

As I wrapped up research on the stories of my second book Historic Haunts of the South and waited eagerly for its release, I finally found the time to keep my vow and research the stories and history of the building a little more thoroughly. What I discovered and found myself asking was whether the paranormal activity in the building could be attributed to the history, specific spirits, the land, or all the artifacts inside? Regardless of what direction I found myself leaning, one thing I knew was that paranormal occurrences happen here on a frequent basis!

After studying the history I learned that the museum was built in 2006, on property that once housed private residences. In fact, the area that makes up the main portion of the museum today was once a private residence from the mid-1940's. A structure which strangely disappeared from the records in 1960. A Mrs. McCormick started a beaches archive in a small building on the property and gave the land and the building to the museum.

Ghostly Activity at the Museum

As for the specific spirits, many paranormal investigation teams have explored the building looking for answers as to why the building is haunted and by whom. Drawn perhaps by the stories of visitors and museum employees and volunteers, Operations

31

Coordinator, Joshua Edwards, for example, has had experiences of his own. He described instances of several days in a row where chairs in the downstairs hallway would move on their own or go completely missing, only to return later to where they were originally supposed to be.

Taryn Rodriguez Boette, who also works at the museum in the archives room has heard many reports of paranormal activity involving the women's restroom upstairs. Known as the green bathroom, ladies have often reported an unnerving and unnatural feeling, especially in the handicap stall. Some describe a feeling akin to that of being watched while in the restroom alone. Adding further to this uncomfortable sensation is the fact that the door has also been known to open and close of its own accord.

Mrs. Boette's interview reminded me of an odd occurrence of my own. While previously researching another location in the archives of the museum for my books, my mom, Gayel Roush, decided to accompany me to see the museum herself. She lived in Jacksonville in the 1960's and visited the beaches often. I didn't tell her anything about the alleged ghost stories and was curious to see if she felt anything on her own. When I was done researching my story she came up to me and said, "That upstairs bathroom really wigged me out! You didn't tell me the place was haunted!" I asked her why she felt "wigged out" and she said, "It's just creepy when you're in the restroom and you feel like someone is watching you." I asked her which stall she was in and she told me it had been the handicap one.

While the stories from the visitors and employees were very compelling, I also knew the museum housed many artifacts from the beach's past and that it was possible that something might be holding on to some sort of energy. I explored for myself examining the artifacts, but found inconclusive results. What little evidence I did find led me to believe that there was nothing malicious here, and whatever spirit or spirits were in the building, they were more playful than anything. As I often like to say ghosts-like living people-don't necessarily perform on command. I resigned myself to the fact that I would have to return and continue looking for evidence like so many research groups before me.

If you or your group want to try and experience something paranormal for yourself (and I encourage you to do so), the museum is available to rent for investigations at a very reasonable fee and the money helps keep the museum and archives going. Regardless of the paranormal aspect, I hope all readers will check out the Beaches Museum by day for its rich detailed history of the area and the amazing treasures contained within.

THE MYSTERIOUS REEF LIGHT
Carysfort Reef Light, Key Largo

···

The Tales of Caesar and Florida

The original Carysfort Reef Light was actually a lightship named Caesar. It was built in New York City, but it went aground near Key Biscayne during a storm while being sailed from its port of origin. It was salvaged by wreckers, and taken to Key West, where the owners bought it back and stationed it at Carysfort Reef. It was blown off its station by a storm went aground at one point on the reef and was replaced after five years of service.

The second light ship was named the Florida. After the Seminoles burned down the Cape Florida Lighthouse in 1836, the only remaining navigational light on Florida's coast (between St. Augustine and Key West) was the Carysfort Reef Lightship. That same year Captain John Whalton, who had captained both lightships, was killed by the Seminoles while he and four helpers went ashore on Key Largo. Unfortunately, Captain Whalton's wife and daughter were visiting the station at the time.

In the 1840s, the monies needed for a third light were appropriated by Congress. Carysfort became the third screw-pile lighthouse in the U.S. Erection of the lighthouse proved to be an incredible challenge as the site was under four and a half feet, and the reef was not solid. Eventually large plates were added to the piles to spread the weight of the lighthouse, and the skeleton of the octagonal pyramidal tower took shape. It sits six nautical miles off the east coast of Key Largo and is an iron screw pile foundation, a skeleton octagonal pyramidal tower. This light is painted red and stands 100 feet above the water.

Carysfort Reef is the oldest functioning light of its type in the United States and was completed in 1852. It is named for the HMS Carysfort, a 1766, 20 gun Royal Navy post ship that ran into the reef in 1770. To this day it still guards the coast.

What Haunts Carysfort Reef?

Many believe the ghost thought to haunt the light is the first keeper, Captain Johnson who died at the light in the 1950s. Several witnesses have reported seeing him at the light looking out to sea, an interesting thing to be sure, especially since the balcony and the enclosed circular structure around the light keepers quarters and its railings were removed long ago. Apparently he is still guarding ships at sea in his afterlife, or maybe keeping the ghost ships off the coast safe (there are many of those reported in the area as well, but that is another story).

THE LEGENDARY CAPTAIN TONY'S
Captain Tony's Saloon, Key West

The legendary and infamous Captain Tony's

Situated in the remote, but infamous hamlet of Key West is a bar called Captain Tony's Saloon. Like many sites in Key West this bar has achieved an almost legendary status with its own myths and stories surrounding it. For example, one of the features of this bar is the fact that anytime a celebrity visits, a barstool is added with that patron's name. The bar currently displays stools for visitors Ernest Hemingway, John F. Kennedy, Harry Truman, and many others. It's also said that tossing a quarter into the mouth of the large Jewfish caught and preserved at the bar will allow good luck to follow you until you leave the island. There's a lot of other equally unusual and interesting stories about the bar, but for this author learning about its history and haunts was foremost in my mind.

A Colorful Past

The building now known as Captain Tony's was originally built in 1851 as an ice house that doubled as the city morgue. A terrible hurricane hit the Keys in 1865, with a sea surge that sent ice, fresh corpses and other things adrift in the surge's aftermath. All the bodies disappeared except one, and it was decided that they would create an unofficial burial site. The body was buried, along with a wall surrounding it containing holy water (it is now inside and part of the pool room). In the 1890s Captain

34

Tony's housed a wireless telegraph station, and then in 1912. it was a cigar factory. Later it was home to a bordello and several speakeasies.

In the 1930s, Josie Russell created the original Sloppy Joe's in the building. The bar would become a regular watering hole for Ernest Hemingway. In 1938 the rent was raised by $1 a month (a steep sum for that time) and Russell decided to move Sloppy Joe's to its current location.

Through the years there have been several different owners and the bar continued to expand. The pub expanded to build around and encompass the wall with the holy water and a hanging tree. This tree was reportedly the site of at least 18 people being hung, 17 for piracy and one for murder! The murderess hung on the tree committed the grisly slayings of her husband and two sons, even serving the chopped up parts of the bodies to backyard animals to devour. A neighbor noticed and brought it to the attention of the town. The crowd found this killer still covered in blood wearing a blue dress. They exacted swift punishment as they dragged her to the hanging tree and she became another on the list who had been hung from its branches.

In 1958 Captain Tony Tarracino bought the place and turned it into Captain Tony's. Jimmy Buffett got his start here in the 1970s and was paid in Tequila. Buffet immortalized the bar and Captain Tony in the song "Last Mango in Paris". Many other noteworthies have called this establishment home including Tennessee Williams, Truman Capote and Bob Dylan.

During additional expansion efforts in 1983, some of the aged plywood flooring was pulled up to reveal the remains of between eight and fifteen bodies. Captain Tony's has placed a skeletal reminder of the find on display behind the bar. It was also during this discovery that the grave marker of a young woman named Elvira was unearthed and now remains exposed in the cement beside a billiard table.

Tony Tarracino sold the place in 1989, but it still retains its name as Captain Tony's. He frequented the bar afterwards especially on Thursdays. Tarracino died in November of 2008 and some believe he is still there. He lived an interesting life as a boat captain, gun runner, gambling casino operator, and former Mayor of Key West. Death might be just too boring for him.

The Spirits at the Bar

With its rich and varied history and all the events that have occurred here, there are several things that could be the cause for any particular paranormal activity. Many believe the bar is haunted because of the hanging tree which still stands in the middle of the bar. While the count of the dead hung from the this tree is believed to be closer to eighteen, there are some who have suggested as many as 75 people may have lost their lives stretched by the neck from its branches. The residual energies from such traumatic events could easily explain the paranormal activity in the bar.

Some locals think the ghost of Elvira is haunting the bar. They point to the grave/headstone that can still be seen in the bar. She died in 1822 and her headstone says "Daughter of Joseph & Susanna Edmunds". She was only 19 years, 8 months, and several days old when she passed. It has been suggested that she may be the spirit that guests encounter in the ladies room. Doors have been known to open and close by themselves and even lock on their own accord.

Besides Elvira, another grave that resides inside the bar is of Reba Sawyer. She was reportedly having an affair and she and her lover would often meet at the bar. After her untimely death, her husband found out about the affair. So, he removed her headstone from the cemetery and dumped it in front of the bar. Tarricino brought the headstone inside and kept it.

The improvised burial site that resulted from the disastrous Key West hurricane could also be a reason for the high number of paranormal reports. While Tony had the bones placed within a cement foundation with bottles of holy water in a make shift vault, this may not have ended the activity. This could be a reason for the numerous reports of cold spots and haunted activity here. In fact, despite the lack of obvious explanation for the temperature difference, the pool room is said to be several degrees cooler that the other rooms. I experienced this first hand when I came to visit Captain Tony's for myself. I looked into the other reports as well, but at that time found only some unusual readings. I didn't experience many of the other activity that haunts this drinking establishment, but may when I return in the future.

Captain Tony's "blue-lady" is perhaps the most legendary and reported of all the bar's haunts. Numerous reports describing apparitions and moving blue blurs have been made. Many patrons have even claimed to photograph the spirit of this former killer and victim of the hanging tree. She is among the most discussed and reported spirits active at this popular Key West bar.

For tourists visiting the area Captain Tony's is a landmark of Key West and a must see spot. How often can you go somewhere with buried bodies, headstones, and a hanging tree all in one spot while you sip on an ice cold soda or indulge in a "spirit" of your own. For fans of the paranormal, this is one Historic Haunt full of history and atmosphere that requires further investigation.

THE GHOSTLY CHILDREN OF ST. PAUL'S
St. Paul's Episcopal Church, Key West

St. Paul's Episcopal Church at night

A church was erected in Key West to service the faithful Episcopal followers. The original church was built between 1838 and 1839 and was constructed of coral rock. It was 38 feet by 58 feet and was impressive. It was destroyed on October 11th, 1846 by a hurricane.

The second church was a wooden structure measuring 28 feet by 66 feet and was consecrated on January 4th, 1851. In 1857 a rectory was erected at the corner of Duval and Eaton streets. Reverend Osgood E. Herrick was the first of a long line of rectors. Again, the church was destroyed, but this time by the Great Fire of Key West in March of 1886. The rectory was spared from the devastation.

A third church was built and completed in 1887 and was slightly bigger than the last one. Yet again, a hurricane struck in October of 1909 and leveled the church, but once again the rectory survived. Later, in 1914, the rectory was moved to its current location and a fourth church was built. It opened its doors on June 8th, 1919 and is the St. Paul's Episcopal church you see today.

In 1991 a major restoration project took place to save the building and restore it to its original beauty. As many paranormal fans know restoration projects have a way of stirring things up. From some of the reports made during this time and after it would seem that this church and the surrounding area are haunted. From my experienced here, the church was filled with the Holy Spirit, but the church yard and the buildings surrounding it…that was a different story.

37

St. Paul's Haunts

The church land was donated many years ago by the widow of John Fleming under the condition that his remains would never be moved from the garden. Her wishes were honored but no one knows exactly where Mr. Fleming is buried. There are reports that his spirit is still there and seems very unhappy with visitors even chasing people away. There have also been reports of the smell of tobacco smoke when he is present.

Ghostly children have also been encountered huddling near the angel statue in the churchyard. Many years ago, a former preacher accused his wife of cheating on him in the building that once stood across the alley. He decided to set the building on fire with her and her lover in it...or so he thought. What he didn't know is she was meeting in the building with the children of the congregation and not a lover. The woman and the children all died in the fire.

There are many reports detailing the children's voices being heard in the churchyard and seeing strange mist hovering over the graves. Mysterious fires have occurred for years where that building once stood.

Many years ago while visiting Key West, my parents and I were walking the streets after the bars were closed and something drew us to the graveyard behind the church. We thought we heard a child sniffling or crying and there was a strange fog over the graves. As we got closer, the sound diminished and the fog disappeared.

St. Paul's Episcopal Church is an interesting building. Even if you don't experience anything paranormal here, it is a beautiful resting spot while visiting Key West. I encourage paranormal fans to check it out themselves and maybe pay their respects to the children.

THE SPIRITS OF SEVEN MILE BRIDGE

Seven Mile Bridge, Marathon

In the late 1800's the face of Florida would forever be changed by Henry Morrison Flagler, founder of Standard Oil and owner of several grand hotels in Florida. In 1880 he decided to provide his well-to-do hotel guests with the most modern form of travel, a train! His plan involved a system of tracks that would run from Jacksonville all the way to Key West.

With Key West more than 100 miles off the coast, Flagler had to build bridges to get from island to island to reach his target destination. One of the bridges built was an amazing seven miles long! This was a pretty rare length for bridges at the time.

Seven Miles of Fun

Flagler's dream was a smashing success. The trains were running smoothly and guests loved the experience of riding a locomotive through the state and over the islands, that is until 1935 when the Labor Day hurricane hit. Floridians, aware of the devastating power of these types of weather conditions were doing everything they could to get to the mainland before the hurricane hit. Escaping the storm's wrath by car and train seemed like a good idea until the worst part of the storm hit the Seven Mile Bridge with cars on the motor bridge and a train on the train bridge. The aftermath of the storm was devastating. The bridges were destroyed and over 400 people were missing.

With the incredible destruction it was decided that East Coast Railway would not be rebuilt. Monroe County bought the damaged tracks in 1938 and converted them into a two lane unbroken highway, known as US1.

The Supernatural Seven Mile

Almost immediately after the hurricane swept through, strange things started to occur in the region of the bridge and are still reported to this day. People have frequently reported driving across the Seven Mile Bridge and claiming to see a train light coming towards them. Many also claim to hear the eerie sound of a train whistle at night. Others report seeing the headlights and hazy details of old motor cars coming their way or driving off the bridge. There have even been reports describing apparitions of people in the water below crying out for help.

This stretch of Florida road is lonely enough and creepy enough at night. While I haven't experienced the spectral locomotive myself, I can just imagine what it would be like to see a train coming right towards you, then vanishing. No doubt it would leave a lasting impression just as the Labor Day hurricane has done to the area. The Seven Mile Bridge incident in Marathon is a terrible reminder of the destructive power of nature and a lesson that perhaps incidents like these storms can act as a focusing point, concentrating the death and destruction into a repeating paranormal reminder.

THE EERIE CRANE CREEK BRIDGE
Downtown Melbourne Crane Creek Train Bridge, Melbourne

photo courtesy State Archives of Florida, Florida Memory

In 1894 during an expansion of the Florida East Coast Railway, a train bridge was added near downtown Melbourne, Florida to help open routes to West Palm Beach. The bridge crosses Crane Creek and locomotives passing over it can completely cross the river in approximately 7 seconds. Not a lot of time to be sure and unfortunately, the reason perhaps for the many tragic deaths tied to this bridge.

The Crane's Tragic Incidents

As far back as the 1920's, people have died on the Crane Creek Bridge. Whether these people were merely walking on the tracks and caught unaware, or chose to try to race the train is uncertain. In addition to its relatively short span, the bridge sits above a 25 foot drop into a 10 foot deep river known to be infested with alligators. The bridges perilous position above the hostile alligators might help explain why so many have tried to make it across the the bridge rather than jump. Two women died on the bridge in 1922 and more recently three girls passed in 2010. Witnesses claimed in both cases that the victims seemed to be unable to hear the train coming or see it on the tracks.

A Haunted Reputation

Locals have said for years that the area is full of negative energy. Some, who have dared to walk the tracks of Crane Creek Bridge, claim that doing so gives you an even heavier and more pronounced feeling of dread. Other common reports of paranormal activity tied to the bridge describe the feeling on or near the tracks of being watched by unseen eyes. There are numerous individuals who claim to have photographs that contain orbs.

I used to live near railroad tracks and could always hear the eerie sound of the train whistle and feel the vibrations. I enjoyed walking along the tracks looking for flattened pennies or laying some down to be flattened. Its hard to believe that victims of the Crane Creek span couldn't hear the whistle or feel the upcoming locomotive on the tracks, but who knows. Florida is in fact #4 in the nation for train pedestrian deaths. So its hard to say whether this span of bridge off the Indian River near US1, is haunted or merely a spot pedestrians need to avoid at all costs!

APPARITIONS AT THE ROSSETTER HOUSE

Rossetter House, Museum, and Gardens, Melbourne

Rossetter House photo courtesy wikimedia commons

The Rossetter, Roesch, and Houston families helped make Melbourne and Eau Gallie what they are today. The collected Rossetter Museum area is a testament to the sacrifices and forethought of these early Florida pioneers. The Rossetter Museum grounds includes; the 1908 James Wadsworth Rossetter House and Gardens, the 1901 William P. Roesch House, and the 1865 Houston Family Memorial Cemetery.

Details on some of the families

The nearby Houston Pioneer cemetery marks the graves of some of the early pioneers and settlers of this historic Eau Gallie area of Florida. Including Sam Houston and his family. Eau Gallie was founded in the 1850s and was home to many sugar cane plantations, rice, and citrus groves and in 1893 it became the southern end of Henry Flagler's Florida East Coast Railway.

William Roesch another prominent early member of this community was the neighbor of James Rossetter. Roesch served as postmaster, newspaper publisher and the city's first mayor.

The Rossetter family arrived in Eau Gallie in 1902 and made their living on the frontier from Jacksonville to the south along the St. Johns River. They were deeply connected to the St. Johns as far back as the colonial era. James Rossetter raised five children and he became the leading merchant in the fishing industry and an agent for

41

Standard Oil Company.

Rossetter died in 1921 and his oldest daughter Carrie P. Rossetter took over the family home and oil distribution business. Seventy years later, Carrie and her sister Ellas, worked to preserve the family home and keep their family history alive.

Paranormal incidents on site

All three buildings on the property are said to be haunted, but the Rossetter House, from reports, seems to be the most haunted. An apparition of a woman has been seen in the foyer and has even been known to speak to visitors in "her" home. On one occasion an EVP was captured in which her spirit was believed to have said "There's too much commotion in my house." Perhaps she just doesn't like large groups of people traipsing through her former home. Can you blame her?

Many people believe that the spirit of Samuel Houston is still in the area as well, especially at the family cemetery where he is buried. Witnesses in the area have reported hearing a disembodied voice whisper the name Sam.

One witness filming the area at night reportedly captured strange light anomalies on film moving around the property. Apparently there are many spirits attached to the property. With so many personal objects in the buildings, the buildings themselves, and the cemetery, there is no wonder the area is haunted. It seems as they all have stayed where they were happiest in life.

A SPIRITED COLONY
Colony Theater, Miami
··

The beautiful art deco style theater opened its doors on January 25th, 1935 in the heart of South Beach as part of Paramount Pictures movie theatre chain. This "beauty queen" is a beloved part of the Miami art deco scene and can be found in Miami Beach's upscale pedestrian Lincoln Mall. Unlike many of the theaters throughout the U.S. The Colony was never allowed to sink into disrepair. It has evolved and enjoyed renovations on several occasions, making it better suited to serve its patrons and the art-loving community of Miami Beach. It recently went through another $6.5 million renovation/restoration to return it to its original grandeur.

When the Colony Theater reopened its doors, after the last renovations, it not only hosted; music, dance, opera, comedy, performance arts, and film, but it had something new to offer, apparently all the work done stirred up a ghost or two.

The Colony's Haunts

Footsteps have often been heard rushing around backstage at the Colony as if things were being prepared and made ready for a performance. Sounds like props and lighting being moved are encountered when the theater is empty, but when anyone goes to investigate, there's no one there. Spot lights have also been known to turn themselves on and off by themselves. They've even turned on when there was no power running to them.

People have also heard ghostly conversations taking place backstage. No one can ever tell what is being said they just hear people carrying on a conversation. When they try to see if anyone is there, they discover they are completely alone. Many believe this to be a stage hand or past employee still continuing to prepare for the shows.

Employees hate closing the theater down by themselves because they get creeped out by the voices and other strange sounds they hear coming from the stage area. An apparition has also been spotted on more than one occasion in this same area. Employees also claim to have issues when locking up for the night. When they turn back around to double check things, lights will frequently be on that they know they turned off. The employees also confided in me that there may be spirits of animals at the Colony as well.

When I was there in 2009 interviewing people for the story I didn't experience a single thing at the Colony. Maybe the spirits knew I was looking for them? I hope to get back and try to learn more about the resident spirits of this Historic Haunt.

The Colony Theater

43

GLEASON'S GHOST AT THE MIAMI THEATER
...HOW SWEET IT IS!

Fillmore Miami Beach at The Jackie Gleason Theater, Miami

History of the Fillmore
The story of the Fillmore at Jackie Gleason Theater in Miami Beach began in 1950 and people came from around the globe to catch the entertainment that appeared here. The theater hosted a variety of events from shows to song and dance, comedy to boxing, all found their

The Fillmore Miami Beach

way to the event card. Sometimes, however, the bigger show was the A-listers, Golden Era Legends, and celebrities in attendance. Everyone from Bob Hope to Jack Benny and Frank Sinatra found their way to the Filmore. On many occasions it was a glamorous site for The Rat Pack to swing at.

During the 1960s while the television boom was it its peek many shows were filmed here at the theater. The Dick Clark Show and the Ed Sullivan Show, were of the biggest shows filmed here. Then in 1964 the city of Miami offered Jackie Gleason the opportunity to film his show here.He agreed and moved his show to sunny Miami. It was a decision that would please Mr. Gleason as he called Miami Beach audiences the greatest in the world.

The theatre was renovated in the 1970s and broadway shows regularly came to play, shows featuring the likes of; Eartha Kitt, Robert Goulet, Joel Grey, Rex Harrison, and many others. The 1980s brought more memorable performances with celebrities like Mickey Rooney, Joel Gray, and several famous classical musicians. The theater would forever reflect the contributions of Jackie Gleason when the city of Miami Beach renamed it in recognition in 1987. The amazing talent continued to pour through the theater doors as the 90s brought Rent, Riverdance, Marc Anthony, Tony Bennett, Liza Minnelli, Seal, and Lenny Kravitz among others.

In 2007 the theater was reborn yet again, reinventing itself as it had done more than once through the years, this time it was a multi-million dollar transformation. Today the theater still hosts some of the biggest names in the entertainment business, combining the rich traditions of days gone by and the energy and passion of Miami Beach and today's performers.

44

The Haunts of the Gleason Theater

Several stage workers have reported that the theater is full of paranormal energy from the past. One past employee claimed that workers would hear sounds coming from the cat walk on a regular basis and that would occasionally drop from that area, even when no one was around. The apparition of a man in white overalls has also been walking on the cat walk. Apparently one of the former stage hands has return to his duties even in his afterlife.

In addition to the ghostly stage hand, there are reports of people feeling slightly lightheaded in the backstage area. Former stage hand describe activity that would lead many to think a vortex might be present in the backstage area. If so, spirits traveling in and out through this location, might not be that unusual. A woman in white has also been seen on the stage after the theater has closed. Her origin and name are unknown. In most cases when someone approached her, she vanished before their eyes.

Ghost of Jackie Gleason ("How Sweet it Is")

Last and certainly not least on this ghostly show of shows is the reported presence of the great one's ghost Jackie Gleason himself (how sweet it is). While Mr. Gleason's ghost hasn't been encountered as often as the other apparitions, it has been seen enough to have been identified. In fact, his lively spirit brings back memories of yesteryear and thrills the local ghost tours. Even if your not a Jackie Gleason fan the theatre is truly a sight to behold. Don't miss it if you are in Miami.

THE SNAKE WARRIOR LIGHTS
Snake Warrior's Island National Park, Miramar
· ·

The Snake Warrior's Island National Park is known as the home for the Great Florida Birding and Wildlife Trail. It consists of 53.3 acres of natural beauty and pleasant hiking trails. Fans of bird watching frequent the sight and make it among the most popular in Florida, but this area holds more secrets than just the remnants of old and new nests and flying animals.

The History of Snake Warrior Island

Archaeologists working at this site have found prehistoric materials during excavations. This evidence has led them to believe that there may have been societies and cultures dating as far back as approximately 500 B.C.E. through approximately AD 1200 to 1000. Further, during research on the area, archaeologists found a camp site of the Miccosukee, a federally recognized Native American Tribe, that were in fact until the mid-20th century part of the Seminole nation.

Historical records from over a century ago indicate that the leader of this tribe was Chitto Tustenuggee (known as the Snake Warrior). Chitto was designated by Chief Sam Jones/Abiaka as his successor during the Second Seminole War. These, during the time between 1835 and 1842 when the U.S. Government troops clashed with various groups of Native Americans were collectively known as the Seminoles.

Historians have identified this area as one of the earliest Seminole settlements in the eastern Everglades which had been occupied for decades before Indian inhabitants were attacked and fled in 1841. Accounts from soldiers at the time, either in writing or by oral tradition, say there were two towns, two dancing grounds, and a council lodge all in this area.

Interestingly, locals in this area claim that Cuban ranchers could be found on the island a full century before the Indians. These early ranchers were known to engage in raising hogs, cattle, and making rum from palmetto berries. These older legends even claim that Native Americans in the early 1800's wouldn't set foot on the island.

There are also strange tales of the area dated to the 1920s and 30s. Most of these tales involve a very eccentric hermit who lived on the island at this time. His interactions with the local populace were sporadic and unusual at best according to most claims.

Regardless of the truth of the early claims, in 1947, Ferry Farms acquired the land and maintained it as pasture land in an attempt to preserve the area. During this time it also saw duty as a dairy farm and citrus grove. It was later purchased in 1992 by the state of Florida through the Emergency Archaeological Property Acquisition Fund.

The Snake Warrior Lights

There have been many peculiar reports from this area late at night. Eerie beams of light have been witnessed by many shooting up towards the sky and are known in verified reports from as long ago as the 1890s. The descriptions of the Snake Warrior rising lights would seem to eliminate the possibilities of swamp gas, or other naturally occurring phenomenon.

Details involving the sighting of apparitions have also been recorded here. Apparitions have been sighted since the 1920s. Many believe these apparitions could be the spirits of the Native Americans who once lived in the area.

Whether the area is haunted or not, it is undoubtedly spooky, especially at night. Those intrepid adventurers with a warrior's spirit may discover it is a great location to explore while in this part of the sunshine state. It is definitely one of the more unusual Historic Haunts.

PARANORMAL PARTY AT THE LAKESIDE INN
Lakeside Inn, Mount Dora, Florida

Lakeside Inn main building

Lakeside Inn's most historic building was opened in 1883 and only consisted of 10 rooms in the two story structure. It was known as the Alexander House and was located practically next door to the railroad station which made it very convenient for the travelers.

The inn sold in 1893 and was renamed the Lake House. The wrap around veranda was a favorite meeting spot for everyone because it had such an amazing view overlooking Lake Dora.

The building was renamed yet again in 1903 to its current incarnation, the Lakeside Inn. The inn had a bit of a shady past during the 1920s when it was a rather popular speakeasy during prohibition. Even today, the trap door used during the inn's checkered past can be seen by lifting the rug in front of the front desk. It leads down into the basement and that is where all the excitement took place and the liquor could be found.

Known Spirits at the Inn

One of the spirits said to still haunt the Lakeside Inn is former owner Charles Edgerton. He bought the building in 1924 and owned it for 55 years. He is the one responsible for all the additions, the swimming pool, and the two newer buildings, The Terrace and The Gables.

Many people claim to have seen Mr. Edgerton in the main building and throughout the property. In 1930, President Calvin Coolidge dedicated the new buildings during his post retirement at the inn. One room is even known as the Coolidge Suite. Besides former presidents, Thomas Edison, Henry Ford, and Dwight D. Eisenhower have also all been guests at this magnificent Inn.

48

Historic Haunts Joins the Party

In October of 2012 Historic Haunts Investigations was asked to join Orlando based American Ghost Adventures on an investigation of The Lakeside Inn. We were happy to oblige, but concerned with the huge turn out for this public investigation. Recording evidence of the paranormal is no exact science to begin with and the addition of extra living bodies whose movements, coughs, whispers, discussions, and other actions can all be caught by recording devices makes sorting through evidence much more of a challenge. However, this group was very serious about cooperating and investigating and many had brought high end ghost hunting equipment of their own.

This equipment would come in handy as the spirits at the inn seemed ready to have us join the party. We learned on the tour that The Lakeside Inn was once a speakeasy and in fact the hidden door to get to this area was under a rug by the main desk in the lobby. The tour headed to the basement to check out this hidden prohibition feature for ourselves. Multiple flashlights, REM pods, EVP recorders, and other devices were put in position. Our initial questions and comments to the spirits were met with little to no reaction. It wasn't until we started to discuss fine cigars, poker, flappers, and booze that we got intense reactions. REM pods all over the room lit up colorfully, K2s, Mel Meters, and flashlights came alive and EVP recorders captured sounds. While one part of the tour group in one area was having success getting the excitable spirits to activate specific colors on the REM pods, another was getting successful responses to questions with the flashlights. Just outside the room in the hall, a few tour group members and guides from American Ghost Adventures had even begun a lengthy question and answer session with a spirit they later learned was the bouncer or the old speakeasy. For the better part of an hour, we were all treated to some of the best responses and captured evidence by equipment that we'd had the pleasure to experience. As the spirits and responses seemed to die down the group separated into smaller segments to explore individual rooms thought to have a lot of paranormal activity.

My husband Deric and I joined the group heading to another area of the inn. There is a story at Mount Dora about a little girl that drowned in the nearby lake. There seems to be some connection between the spirits in this room and the little girl. When we began asking questions in this room about the little girl Deric and I both saw the K2 EMF meters fluctuate wildly (and well away from electrical sources). We also experienced a subtle electrical charge in the room like you might experience before an impending thunder storm. We experienced a few other odd occurrences during this visit, but nothing that rivaled the activity in the room or the basement.

Historic Haunts Returns

Historic Haunts Investigations was invited to investigate here again in February 2013 with American Ghost Adventures (AGA) out of Orlando. I brought three of my team members with me this time to work with AGA and we all had a fairly eventful night.

While we were investigating the Coolidge Room my EVP Specialist/Investigator Eric O'Dierno who was right next to me on my right and I experienced a strange cold spot out of nowhere with no air vent or window to explain it. My Interviewer/ Investigator, Jolyn O'Dierno, who was to my left felt it as well and commented on it.

Strangely, just as she voiced her comments my full spectrum camera died and Eric's equipment faltered as well. A split second before the equipment failed, I heard a very strange noise on my real time RTEVP recorder. It was an unexplainable sound, but just as I heard it all the equipment failed.

Later during the investigation while in a two room suite, my Tech Advisor/Investigator Deric Pearce and Eric went into the adjoining room from where we were and asked a few question about the little girl who drowned on the lake. They didn't obtain any details but the spirit that interacted with them in the room was a male, it seemed to know of the little girl's death, but when the team asked the spirit if he was responsible for it they didn't get a reply either way.

During a previous investigation here at the inn Deric and I both felt an electrical charge when we spoke about the little girl on the lake. At the same time we felt this we had a spike on the K2 EMF Meter.

Also during our initial investigation while we were in the basement we had a ton of activity as if the party was still going on. We had reactions from all the equipment until we mentioned the bouncer. As soon as we asked about his everything went off. I think at that point the party was over.

If you want to have a fantastic, relaxing, and paranormal experience at the Lakeside Inn, book a room when American Ghost Adventures has an investigation going on. Go to their website www.americanghostadventures.com and get your tickets for the investigation, then book your room. You will be in for a paranormal treat.

Ting Rappa co-owner of AGA has been doing paranormal investigation tours since 2004 and says, "Come where the paranormal is normal. American Ghost Adventures was founded on the premises of bringing the ordinary person into an environment that is extraordinary."

For more info on the inn go to: http://lakeside-inn.com/

SPECTRAL SEMINOLES AND THE SUGAR MILL
Cruger de Peyster Plantation Sugar Mill Ruins, New Smyrna

Cruger de Peyster Plantation Sugar Mill Ruins

Florida's Early Sugar Interests

During the 1800's there was a strong interest throughout Florida in establishing sugar mills to provide a local source for this popular commodity. Most of these ventures were dismal failures or mediocre successes. In the 1830's the Cruger de Peyster Plantation and Sugar Mill was one of the more interesting failures.

The Plantation's History

Built in 1830 from coquina rock which was quarried nearby, the Cruger de Peyster Plantation would only see a few years of operation before it and the nearby saw mill would cease production. In December 1835 several buildings surrounding the property and the mills themselves were destroyed by Seminole Indians after running off the overseers. Much of the buildings, including the mills were demolished or burned down. The site was altered further by soldiers garrisoned there to keep watch over the hostile Seminole Indians.

The Mills Today and the Paranormal Reports Surrounding It

Today this 17 acre Volusia County historical landmark draws a lot of visitors. Besides the remnants of the walls, many objects and elements from the mill's past remain; including large metal sugar production vats and pieces of the saw mill.

Further, archeological digs uncovered crosses, crucifixes, candle sticks,

The large remnants of sugar production

51

and an altar, making them think there may have been a church there prior to the mill. The sugar mill ruins were added to the U.S. National Register of Historic Places August 12th, 1970.

Many visitors to the ruins have reported the sensation of being watched from the woods, even when completely alone. The spirits of Seminole Indians have often been seen darting through the woods as if the warriors were still fighting their war, especially at night fall. Other witnesses have reported being followed when touring the area by shadow figures. Are the native americans still fighting to keep their land or could it be someone else protecting what they believe is their land? While visiting this unique and photogenic sight, I too felt as if I was being watched from the woods. While I did get some unusual readings from my equipment, nothing dramatic presented itself. I may have to return and scout this Historic Haunt further.

Cruger de Peyster Plantation Sugar Mill Ruins and the possible altar

MANIFESTATIONS AT THE MAFIA HOUSE
The Mafia House, New Smyrna Beach

While in New Smyrna doing research I interviewed several people about haunted locations in town and two places came up in conversation the most; The Riverview Hotel (which was featured in my second book Historic Haunts of the South) and The Mafia House. One woman said that the Mafia House spooked her as a kid and still spooks her as an adult.

The Origins of the Mafia House

John Maeder, an unusual man to say the least, began building his home in 1969 and the rumors about him and his home started long before construction was completed. At 6,000 square feet, with gun turrets on the roof, 10 inch thick steel reinforced concrete walls, bullet proof glass windows, armor plated doors, and a heliport on the roof (among other things) its easy to see why locals referred to this building as "The Mafia House".

The house and its many unusual features figured prominently into the local media coverage. In fact, it became the center of even more attention in 1970 when the owner John Maeder was found dead at the bottom of a 15 foot ravine. Those involved claimed he was riding a tractor over the dunes when it flipped and rolled, crushing his head. It was ruled an "accidental death", but an interesting thing was that if it was "accidental" why did they find three spent bullet casings near his body?

The Ghost at the Mafia House

Many witnesses have reported seeing Maeder's apparition looking out windows and walking along the roof top. Some even stated he appeared to be holding a machine gun. Others have reported mysterious shadow figures moving throughout the property.

Maybe Maeder has some unfinished business he needs to take care of? Or maybe he wants the truth to be known, that perhaps he was really murdered? Regardless, this highly unusual and fortified structure is worth at least a drive-by.

THE MYSTERIOUS TURNBULL RUINS
Turnbull Ruins, New Smyrna Beach
....

The mysterious Turnbull Ruins

One of the more mysterious and interesting paranormal sites in the state of Florida is the Turnbull Ruins. There is a large and growing group of historians and researchers who believe this might be the original sight of Spanish Colonization pre-dating St. Augustine and its "Castillo de San Marco" (see Historic Haunts Florida). Most find some of the details of the ruins, its coquina makeup and building techniques, apparent weapon placements, defensive structural elements, and other details enough to suggest a fort or ship building location. To those in this camp these qualities alone are more than enough evidence to suggest that Spain may have been here before St. Augustine. If not, the lingering questions of who built it remain a mystery.

The Turnbull Ruins measure approximately 40 feet by 80 feet. The ruins are located in Old Fort Park and were constructed with coquina block. The ruins are extremely old.

Turnbull's Early Attempts...What we do Know

In 1768 Dr. Andrew Turnbull arranged for almost 1500 colonists of varying ethnicities to establish a settlement in Florida. After three months of travel they landed in what is now known as New Smyrna Beach. The plan was to found a colony to grow sugar cane, hemp, indigo and other crops. Unfortunately, the colonists had to deal with food shortages, Indian attacks, heat, mosquitoes, and the hardships of intense labor and poor housing. So its no surprise that when Dr. Turnbull tried to get his colonists to build him a large stone mansion in late 1777, they revolted and fled. making their way to St. Augustine. A year later Turnbull left for Charleston and abandoned

54

the colony.

Despite the tales of its early beginnings some historians believe Turnbull came across pre-existing ruins and tried to build his mansion on top of them. Maps of the time don't mention a fort being there, let alone possible weapons placements and a large scale colony.

By 1801, what little remained of Turnbull's colony was scarce. Dr. Ambrose Hull came down from Connecticut with a desire to start a new colony. His plans were thwarted temporarily by an Indian attack, but he regrouped and renamed the area "Mount Olive". Hull hired masons to build his two story home on top of the ruins. They completed their project, but sadly, the home was later destroyed in 1812 by the Patriots War.

Eighteen years later, Thomas Stamps started a sugar plantation on the same site in 1819. It too was somewhat short-lived as it was destroyed not long after in 1835 by Seminole Indians. In 1854, John D. Sheldon built a forty room hotel on the site where the two story home once stood, but it too was destroyed, but this time by the opposing forces of the Civil War.

Turnbull's Haunts

Turnbull is a very active location. There are many paranormal reports made involving incidents and entities spotted around the ruins. One commonly recurring report involves the spirit of an apparently 16th Century Spanish Soldier. He is always seen walking the grounds and staring out towards the water. He performs as if continuing his duties of standing watch and is suggestive of a residual haunt.

Others incidents reported involve strange noises especially late at night, and the sensation of being followed while walking around the grounds.

Maybe one day the historians and archeologists will get down to the bottom of things and be able to determine what all has taken place here and who's spirits might still remain. The activity around the Turnbull is particularly interesting because of its history or lack thereof. The presence of apparitions of 16th century soldiers would suggest that perhaps there was a fort here and an early part of history we are missing.

The Turnbull Ruins remain a mystery

THE PARANORMAL AND PUBLIC ENEMY NUMBER 1

Barker-Karpis Gang House, Ocklawaha

In 1935 Kate Blackburn rented a lakefront house in Marion County, Ocklawaha, Florida where she and her family could vacation. The towns people couldn't help but feel something was odd about her and her family. Little did they know that the vacationing "family" was none other than Arizona "Ma" Barker and her sons. Together they made up part of the notorious Barker-Karpis Gang.

Ma Barker and the Gang

Ma Barker was the FBI's Public Enemy #1. She and her four sons, Herman, Lloyd, Fred and Arthur, abandoned by their father George (who ran out on them) engaged in a crime spree throughout the midwest. These crimes included multiple accounts of murder, highway robbery, bank robbery, kidnapping, cashing stolen checks, and other serious offenses. The gang had brought some serious heat on themselves in the last few years with high profile kidnappings including William Hamm of the Hamm's Brewery family, and Edward Bremmen (a prominent Minnesota banker whose dad was a close friend of President Franklin Roosevelt). The deaths of several policemen during some of their crimes also kept them foremost in the FBI's minds. Associating with and traveling in circles that included "Shotgun George" Ziegler, Chicago Mobster Frank Niti and the infamous John Dillinger only helped the their reputation spread. To the gang the house in Ocklawaha seemed as good as any to lay low.

Laying Low on Ocklawaha

Unfortunately, they weren't very good at "laying low". The gang vacationed by wasting away the hours playing cards, drinking alcohol, and fighting amongst themselves, which drew some attention from the townsfolk. In addition, the gang had been interested in a large gator in nearby Lake Weir that everyone called "Gator Joe, and some gang members were reportedly witnessed trying to shoot the animal with "Tommy Guns". Ironically, it wasn't any of this loud and over the top behavior that led their enemies to them, it was a letter sent by Ma Barker to one of her missing sons, Arthur "Doc" Barker telling him about the gator that sealed the fate of her and her son Fred.

Arthur Barker was arrested in Chicago on January 8th. The FBI were tipped off to Ma Barker's location when they tracked the letters he had received from his mother to her vacation spot. Acting on that tip they mobilized and prepared to capture the remaining members of the gang. What the FBI didn't know was the fact that most of the other gang members had left 3 days before, leaving only Ma Barker and Fred at the vacation home.

A Record Shoot-Out

FBI agents surrounded the house, and ordered them to surrender reportedly shouting, "Unless you come out, we're going to start shooting!" To which Ma Barker reportedly replied, "Go ahead!" What followed was an intense hours-long gun battle (one of the longest in FBI history) during which over 2,000 shots were fired! Many locals allegedly watched the firefight, even holding picnics during the gun play.

After gunfire ceased from inside the building, Willie Woodbury (a local estate handyman) was ordered to enter the premises with a bullet-proof vest. Woodbury found everyone inside dead. Both Ma and her son Fred were found dead in the upper left bedroom of the house. Fred's body lay riddled with bullets, Ma Barker's had only a single bullet wound. According to the FBI reports they found a Tommy Gun laying in her hands as well as approximately $10,000 in cash in her pockets.

After the Shoot-Out

J. Edgar Hoover claimed to the press that she was,"the most vicious, dangerous criminal brain of the last decade." However, many historians now believe Ma Barker was merely an accomplice and that Hoover's remarks were a way to avoid public out-cry for the gunning down of a 61 year old woman. Interviews of other Barker-Karpis gang members claim she "couldn't plan breakfast" let along play an active role in criminal activity. After her death, Ma Barker's long lost husband George turned up long enough to try to claim the cash found on her body.

Over the next few years the remaining members of the gang were mostly captured or killed. Arthur "Doc" Barker was killed trying to escape Alcatraz in January 1939. Ironically, his brother Lloyd was released from prison a year earlier in 1938 and served as a U.S. Army cook during World War II, even earning a Good Conduct medal and being Honorably Discharged before being killed later by his wife.

The Property and Reports of the Paranormal

Until recently, the town of Ocklawaha performed a re-enactment of the infamous shoot-out every January, and tales are still told at the nearby "Gator Joes" restaurant. Many repairs have been made to the house over the years, but the bullets have been left wedged into the building, and some of the original furniture that was present the day of the shoot-out. In 2012 the property was up for sale with a minimum suggested bid of $1 Million. It remains private property today.

Locals claim that the house is still haunted and local reports of paranormal activity seem to back that up. Witnesses claim to have seen a stern-faced woman looking out the windows when the house was known to be empty. Many believe Ma is keeping an eye out for the FBI. Other persistent reports describe furniture moving and voices heard at night. While in other limited reports witnesses claimed to have encountered the sounds of multiple gun shots on the anniversary of the shoot-out, most reports describe the sounds of a rowdy poker game with fighting and yelling.

Interestingly enough in the 1970s a medium went through the home. She claimed to have successfully convinced Fred Barker's spirit and some of the others to leave. Ma Barker's spirit reportedly refused. Whether you experience the paranormal when in the neighborhood or not, you have to appreciate this historic landmark from the days of Public Enemy #1

LAKE EOLA'S GHOST DOG
Lake Eola, Orlando

Scenic Lake Eola

Lake Eola in downtown Orlando is a beautiful place. In fact, I thought it was such a pretty location that I chose to get married there. It's not only a peaceful spot filled with swans and an abundance of flowers and trees, it is also known to be haunted.

A Loyal Friend Until the End

Many years ago, as the story goes, a little brown terrier dog was abandoned by its owner on the eastern side of the lake. The dog was put into a bag and thrown into the lake to drown. A steep price to pay for being loyal and loving its master.

Man's Best Supernatural Friend

There have been many reports from many different people and visitors to the lake that have described a little brown dog roaming the shoreline then vanishing before their eyes. Others have reported hearing the sounds of a small dog barking coming from the eastern side of the lake. When these Lake Eola visitors investigated further they were surprised to find no dogs present. Still, we couldn't help but wonder could this be an old legend or a true story? I can only share the details of my most recent trip to Lake Eola, my wedding. Even though we didn't discover any signs of the ghost dog during our wedding, it doesn't mean he wasn't there.

Take a walk around this gorgeous lake and see if you see the little dog for yourself.

NEGLECTED HAUNTS
OF THE SUNLAND HOSPITAL
Sunland Hospital Grounds,
Pine Hills Area of Orlando

Old postcard with aerial view of Hospital

Caring for the sick and needy is a noble pursuit. Many in the field begin with the best of intentions. Unfortunately, sometimes the best of intentions go astray. This was the case at Sunland Hospital.

Sunland's History

Sunland Hospital was also known as "Sunnyland" or "Bellevue Hospital". The hospital was started in 1960 to help people, not abuse them. But lack of funds and staff made the hospital's care go downhill fast. Patients were abused, starved, and many kept in a zombie like state so they wouldn't disturb other patients or staff members.

Many employees of the hospital that were trying to give proper care to the patients were appalled at the conditions and turned the reports of abuse in to hospital higher-ups. Unfortunately, these employees were quickly fired and the allegations were swept under the rug.

Some local groups of children went to the hospital to volunteer to sing to the patients in an attempt to lift the patient's spirits, but most were scared away by what they saw behind the hospital's walls.

One report describing some of the hospitals violations came from a former hospital

59

maintenance man who was sent to do a job and kept hearing someone yelling at him and banging on something. When he finally turned around to see who it was and where it was coming from he saw a patient in a wheel chair whose legs had been amputated. One of the staff members came in to remove the patient and told the maintenance man that he should be glad they had amputated the patient's legs because he used to chase after people. The staff member went on to add "Now he doesn't chase people but he still makes too much noise."

As time went on the stories of abuse and neglect piled up. Patients would be left alone in their beds, cribs, or rooms for hours. They would even sometimes wake up to find a rat in their bed. Some of the patients were unnecessarily fed with feeding tubes due to lack of staff to actually sit with them to feed and chat with them during their meals. Another terrifying report came from the hospital when a night orderly allegedly got a patient pregnant.

By 1978, a Federal Class Action Law Suit was filed by ARC (Association for Retarded Citizens) to stop the abuse and neglect. In 1983 the hospital closed as did its sister hospital in Tallahassee which also had similar reports turned in against them. In 1999 the three story, 350,000 square foot building was torn down and a park was created with very few remnants of the hospital still standing.

What visitors to the site see today at one of the entrance areas

Sunland Hospital's Paranormal Legacy

There have been many reports over the years from dozens of witnesses that would suggest the area where the hospital once stood is haunted. Late at night, people who are taking walks through the area have heard mysterious screams and cries coming from the area. Footsteps have been heard following people in that same locations and strange lights have been seen as well. All of these with no human agents to explain them.

An apparition of a little girl in green has been seen in the area. She appears lost and scared, but when people try to approach her to help she disappears. Some visitors to the area have even reported the smell of illness in the area as if walking through a hospital while still in the park.

There is also a cemetery called Greenwood Cemetery and Memorial nearby. It contains the small headstones of at least 88 of the children who passed away while in the hospital. There have been several reports of unusual occurrences in the area of the cemetery. Some of these reports describe children's voices coming from all around in the area of the graves.

Historic Haunts Investigates

When we visited here in 2013, I couldn't help but be swept up in an overwhelming sense of loss for the children and the other former patients of the hospital. Seeing the rubble down the hill from the park made us realize how big this complex once was. As we walked back up the hill towards the park, I kept feeling as if someone was behind us. I kept turning around expecting to see someone or even and animal but there was no one there. You couldn't escape the sensation that someone was watching us walking around the area. Our equipment picked up varying fluctuations, but nothing substantial.

Its so sad that the spirits of these children and the other patients aren't at peace yet. Its highly unlikely that these spirits will with the hospital gone. Though the beautiful little park has been constructed, and may offer a little comfort to the children's spirits. One can only hope the rest will find solace at some point in their afterlife.

THE MYSTERY LIGHTS OF WASHINGTON OAKS
Washington Oaks Garden State Park, Palm Coast

Washington Oaks Garden State Park
photo courtesy of Mark Avette, wikimedia and creative commons

The garden's early start

Before the Europeans lived in what we now know as Palm Coast, Native Americans lived there. The hill at the top of the Rose Garden was formed due to the oyster shells that were left by the Indians. In 1818 a man from St. Augustine by the name of Jose Mariano Hernandez bought property in the area and named it "Bella Vista". He was a citizen of the Spanish Colony owning land that was granted by Spain.

When Florida became a United States territory, Hernandez swore his allegiance to the new colony and changed his first name from Jose to Joseph and became Brigadier General in command of the militia before and during the Second Seminole War from 1835 to 1842.

During the war, many plantations were burned down by the Seminole Indians but Hernandez's plantation was spared. In 1845, his daughter Luisa married George Lawrence Washington. When Luisa died in 1888, Washington purchased all of Louisa's family property. Louisa's sister and many who live in the area named it "The Washington Place".

Several different owners through the years until 1936, when Louise Powis Clark bought the land for her and her third husband Owen D. Young. It would be their winter home and they called it "Washington Oaks". In 1926 upon Owen's death, Louise donated most of the property to the state of Florida and she specified that the gardens must be "maintained in their present form".

A state park opens and paranormal reports begin

Washington Oaks Garden State Park opened to the public on July 1st, 1964 and ghostly reports have been reported ever since. Some visitors to the area have reported seeing a Spanish gentleman in military garb throughout the property. Others have reported seeing the apparitions of Native Americans.

Most of the reports that come in are of strange lights seen floating over the area and floating throughout at night. There are strange blue or green balls of light that appear and disappear quickly and shoot off at great speeds.

Whether you experience a ghostly ball of light or see an apparition of an ancient soul when visiting here, you are guaranteed one thing, the joy of taking in the beautiful gardens.

PENSACOLA'S PARANORMAL LIGHTHOUSE

Pensacola Lighthouse, Pensacola

The Pensacola Lighthouse

I'm a big fan of lighthouses and all the early efforts of the keepers to protect sailors and keep passengers safe. Lighthouses are picturesque beacons that all too often draw paranormal energies as well as ships. Florida has no shortage of haunted lighthouses, but the Pensacola lighthouse like its cousin in St. Augustine (see Historic Haunts Florida) has been called one of the most haunted lighthouses in America. Obviously the story of the lighthouse belonged in this book.

A Light History

The light ship Aurora Borealis was the first light looking over Pensacola Bay in 1823. She was moved from the mouth of the Mississippi River to Pensacola because they were in need of a light so the sailors could come safely into port. Though congress had appropriated $6,000 in 1823 to fund the construction of a lighthouse in Pensacola, construction did not begin until 1824. The Aurora Borealis would help guard seafarers in Pensacola's harbor until the lighthouse was completed. Frequent rough seas made the need for a light there on the bay an imperative.

This first lighthouse in Pensacola would be lit and began service on December 20th, 1824. Jeremiah Ingraham was the lighthouse's first keeper. Tall trees on Santa Rosa Island made it hard for people at sea to see the only 40 foot tall light that sat on a bluff. Unfortunately, people learned quickly that the lighthouse still didn't reach far enough out to sea or over the tree line, and there were numerous complaints that the light was just too dim.

As a result of the problems with the first tower, a second tower was started in 1858 and was completed and first lit on January 1st, 1859. It stood 159 feet tall which was easily tall enough to be seen over the tree line on Santa Rosa Island. Plus, the new light was on the same 40 foot tall bluff which made the light appear even taller from the ocean as if it were standing 199 feet above sea level.

Unfortunately, keeper Jeremiah Ingraham would pass before the second lighthouse was completed (1840). His wife Michaela would take over as head keeper until 1855 when she handed the title over to her son-in-law Joseph Palmes. He would serve until early 1859 becoming the first keeper of the new Pensacola lighthouse.

In January 1861 Florida seceded from the United States and Union Forces abandoned for Barrancas in favor of Fort Pickens on the western end of Santa Rosa Island. The Confederates then took over the tower and later removed the lenses. The two forces watched each other from either side of the bay until November 22nd, 1861 when a two day exchange of artillery occurred.

While the light was constructed of granite and brick, and granite is very well known for holding energy. The brick held something other than energy. There are over a half dozen rounds of ammo lodged into the bricks of the lighthouse, but only the outer side, there was no damage to the inner walls.

The Confederated forces evacuated the area in May of 1862 at which time it then fell back into Union hands. The lighthouse would see a string of keepers and a few unusual circumstances. In 1875, lightning struck the tower twice, which caused some of the metal fixtures in the tower to melt. Wild ducks flew through the lens room in 1885 damaging the lens. In 1886, George "Tucker" Clifford became head keeper, his tenure would be the longest (31 years). His family would help keep the light as well. Clifford's daughter, Ellen (Ella), would marry Ernest Miller at the lighthouse in 1903. She would die in 1905 from complications five months after giving birth to her daughter Naomi.

The Lighthouse's Paranormal Activity

There are few areas affiliated with the lighthouse that haven't had some sort of paranormal activity. In fact, there is so much activity here that clairvoyants were brought in and confirmed its haunted status. In addition, a popular ghost hunting program also investigated here and seemed to have experiences in-line with the multiple reports by witnesses.

In the main tower itself there have been multiple reports of footsteps and unusual K2 readings. All of these were confirmed and experienced by the televised investigating group. They also researched reported appearances of the apparition of a slave in the basement. They discovered the paranormal activity and reports extended to the keepers house and quarters as well.

Eye witnesses at the keepers house have reported voices and the apparition of a woman in the main quarters. Other reports describe encounters in the keeper's bedroom where a murder was known to have taken place. The ghost of a woman believed to have died from child birth complications has also been seen here. Some believe this latter spirit might be Ella.

Many people believe the person haunting the Pensacola Lighthouse could be its original light keeper, Joseph Palmes. Many of the paranormal occurrences seem to be centered on cold spots and the feeling of being watched.

Historic Haunts Drops in

When I visited here, unfortunately, I discovered the Lighthouse was closed that day. So I roamed around the grounds for some time and the entire time I was there I felt as if someone was watching me from the keeper's quarters. There was no one else around, but there was that distinct feeling that someone was in the keeper's house watching me. I asked the people over at the fort and they said there have been other reports of people feeling like they were being watched when there was no one inside the keeper's house.

SPOOKS FOR SALE
Sandlin House, Punta Gorda

Spooks for Sale
Ever wanted to own a haunted house? Well, here's your chance! The beautiful Sandlin House in Punta Gorda Florida was built in 1893 by successful businessman, James Sandlin. It overlooks Gilcrest Park and is currently listed at $1.59 million (as of May 2014).

The Story of the Home
James Sandlin's 14 year old daughter, Mary Leah, was ironing with a kerosene iron on their beautiful porch one day in 1909 when some kerosene spilled on her dress. Her dress caught on fire and she suffered severe burns from which she eventually passed away. Ever since the young girl's death the house has been haunted.

Sandlin's resident spirit
The home's current occupants have described the paranormal presence in the home as peaceful, but prank-loving. Many people have reported hearing footsteps and the sounds of a rustling petticoat. Doors and windows have opened and closed of their own accord. Some locals who have passed by the house have even seen a woman on the widow's peak when no one living in the house was home. Could this be Mary Leah still enjoying the view and making her presence known?

Now that the house is up for sale, the owners hope that the young ghost will travel on with them since she is such a peaceful presence. They don't mind her tagging along to their new home. Though they've described her as a little prankster at times, they would miss her if she didn't go along with them once the house sells.

67

JUST YOUR FRIENDLY NEIGHBORHOOD HAUNTED ANTIQUE SHOP

Antiques and Uniques Collectibles, St. Augustine

Antiques and Uniques Collectibles

St. Augustine has no shortage of haunted hot spots. Many of these I've covered here and in previous books. Still, there is one situated on an old side street that has drawn much attention from televised ghost shows, investigators, and paranormal authors (like yours truly). That would be St. Augustine's very own Antiques and Uniques Collectibles.

The history of the place

The site is located on Aviles Street, (known to be very haunted) and was once the Los Remedios Catholic Cathedral Cemetery which dates back to the 1700s. The building, now known as Antiques and Uniques Collectibles is situated atop the old cemetery and was originally built between 1885 and 1888 by A.H. Cornish. It was only a one story building at the time of its creation, and was St. Augustine's first city jail with two cells in the back of the building. It was vacated prior to 1893 and was later enlarged and a second floor was added.

Over the years it has been used for office space, a book store, a Chinese laundry, a bait and tackle shop, and several gift stores. It was purchased in 2010 by Larry and Denice Altman who had been traveling to St. Augustine since 2003 and found themselves drawn to the place for years wanting to own it.

Larry and Denice were happy to relocate to St. Augustine and the building they so loved. Little did they know however, that owning an antique store means you sometimes inherit a few resident ghosts. The Altman's paranormal encounters began almost as soon as they began their remodel in preparation for a grand opening. Not only did things get stirred up, they continue even now and happen practically every single day.

Life on the Small Screen

The Altman's have had so many personal experiences that a nationally known paranormal television show featured their biographic, and many paranormal teams have investigated this location. Even my Historic Haunts Investigations team has been allowed to investigate on more than one occasion. Over the last few years my team and I have become good friends of Denice and Larry and somewhat familiar with their resident ghosts.

Historic Haunts drops by and the cameras catch it

Our first trip to the building was just a preliminary visit to see what our impressions were and scope out the location. This visit consisted of a group that included my husband and I, and another small family of tourists and paranormal fans. Shortly after entering the building though we felt as if something was there and our equipment seemed to corroborate. The very first photo I took in the back "closet" room I captured a mist forming in which there appeared to be a face (although this could have been a case of matrixing). Not long after the picture was taken, I felt something touch my shoulder and I told the tour guide something was behind me. A guest on the tour snapped a photo which seemed to show a spirit orb on my shoulder, the same shoulder that was touched.

Denice and Larry are very aware that photographic anomalies occur frequently and have cameras positioned throughout the store. They show a live feed on a daily basis to see if anyone picks up on something they miss. Often people do. In fact, during all of our investigations we have been on this live feed and folks at home frequently spotted unusual phenomenon and activity that we didn't and hadn't captured with our equipment.

The Altman's cameras routinely capture objects moving and other paranormal phenomenon. A clear cooler door (angled to stay closed and sealed to preserve the groceries within) frequently opens on its own, and a spirit orb is often seen floating through the store. This orb has a few unique qualities of its own, it likes to settle on and block out a shelf and sometimes begins to take on features that resemble a small child.

Some of our More Memorable Investigations

When my team investigated in September 2013 we encountered EMF spikes, strange sensations, and flashlight activity which responded to questions. On this particular investigation my husband Deric was here along with two other team members, Eric and Jolyn O'Dierno. While the four of us were in the garage storage area investigating, the door to the store opened on its own. We examined the door closely. There were no vents nearby that could have blown it open, it was not angled or resting in such a way as to open on its own. The door had been closed and shut soundly when we entered the garage. This is not uncommon activity at Antiques and Uniques Collectibles, and a great example of why we've repeatedly come back. This location has thus far never let us down.

During our most recent investigations in April 2014, we encountered the most activity we'd experienced in the building yet. The team that day consisted of myself and Gayel and Jim Roush, Amy and Will Mann, and and this time as they sometimes do Larry and Denice joined us as well. It wasn't long into the investigation before we encountered temperature fluctuations, EMF spikes on the Mel Hybrid, flash light responses to questions, and responses with the spirit box. At one point during the investigation, Amy's hair was pulled and it was caught on the store cameras!

During the spirit box session, Gayel commented that she had never been there before (meaning in the closet/hall area). Right after she said this the spirit box replied, "Have too!" Gayel responded back that she hadn't and the box replied, "Yes you have!" We suggested to Gayel that while she may not have been back in the closet/hall area of the store, she had been in the store and as soon as we said that the spirit box said, "That's right."

The spirit box also clearly stated my name, Gayel, Denice, and Will and answered a few questions. During our time in the smaller room in the back left corner of the store the entire team heard a kitten loudly mewing. We had heard this earlier, a cat meow clearly sounding like it was coming from the middle of the room. We searched diligently for items in the store that might have created a similar noise and for any felines in the surrounding area. There were no cats in the building , nor vicinity so we couldn't debunk that.

As if all this activity wasn't enough we also smelled bacon cooking in the middle of the room. There is no way to cook bacon in the middle of the store (with the exception of the very loud beeping microwave). We searched the store wondering if the smell could have come blowing through any windows. Shortly after we noticed and began to investigate it disappeared. Typically the smell of cooking bacon doesn't disappear that quickly, but lingers.

If you find yourself in St. Augustine (ghost hunting or not) and are looking for a great treasure or a spirit to say hello to, stop by Antiques and Uniques Collectibles and see what you encounter. The Altman's are very friendly and welcoming people, happy to share stories. However, if you want your own unique experience you can pay to investigate the building for a reasonable fee, just ask Denice and Larry. This antique shop is one of my favorite Historic Haunts and one of the few that keeps me coming back.

GHOSTS OF THE MATANZAS
Fort Matanzas, St. Augustine

Fort Matanzas

St. Augustine, Florida is thought by many to be the oldest city in the U.S. Unfortunately, with everyone eager to claim a piece of the new world it was only a matter of time before conflicts would come up. The first conflict in St. Augustine occurred the year it was founded in 1565. Almost 175 years before the construction of Fort Matanzas. Many years ago, a massacre took place in the Matanzas Inlet. Many French Huguenots were murdered and the mass killing is what has given the river its name. Matanzas is the Spanish word for slaughter.

History of the area

King Phillip II of Spain was on the throne during the time of the massacre. Phillip was angry not just because the French has established a colony, and that they were Protestants (Phillip was Catholic) , but also because the Spanish had run ins with Jean Ribault. Ribault was a commander of a large french force that left their settlement near present day Jacksonville (Fort Caroline) to attack the Spanish at their new settlement in St. Augustine.

Phillip sent General Pedro Menendez to get rid of the French, he made the French accept Catholicism as their religion, then began killing them "in the name of God". In the end, over 300 were dead.

71

The Spanish in an effort to end attacks on their interests (especially the British) built Fort Matanzas to help guard St. Augustine's river approach from the South. Florida Governor Montiano had the fort built without the king's permission to ensure St. Augustine's protection and that of the rich shipping lanes coming from the Spanish Caribbean. Fort Matanzas, though small, proved useful as she fired her cannons and drove Oglethorpe and the british back forcing them to retreat, not once, but twice.

In 1821, the U.S. took possession of Fort Matanzas from the Spanish. They were welcomed by ruined interiors and foundations that had cracked. The former St. Augustine settlements would see conflicts with Indians and during the Civil War, Forts Matanzas and Marion (the current Castillo de San Marco) would go from Confederate to Union hands. In a state of disrepair, Fort Matanzas was merely a marker; Union forces actually used a barge stationed in the Matanzas river nearby to successfully stop Confederate blockade runners.

It wasn't until the Henry Flagler era, during the late 19th Century, that the vacationing rich and famous were motivated to speak to their friends and Congressmen about restoring St. Augustine's two dilapidated forts on the Matanzas. Congress voted some small monies toward repair, but it wasn't until the 1920s that President Calvin Coolidge named St. Augustine's forts National Monuments and began extensive repair work. Forts Matanzas and Marion were transferred to the National Park Service in the 1930s.

Haunted stories around the Fort and inlet

There have been many reports over the years of green lights rising above the water near Fort Matanzas. Witnesses claim they seem to dance around then vanish leaving no trace of ever having being there. These glowing green lights are often reported in the woods around Fort Matanzas. Many have even reported seeing the water of the Matanzas River turn blood red during the full moon. In some accounts the blood and waters extend to the beaches near Fort Matanzas giving the sand the same eerie and bloody appearance.

These strange green balls of light and blood red waters have been reported near the now Castillo de San Marcos as well as if they run all the way up the river from fort to fort.

Fort Matanzas itself has also had some paranormal incidents. People claim to hear whispered speech or conversations at the Fort in various places with no people present causing it. Shadow figures are often seen walking around the fort as if they are still on guard.

I have visited both of these forts extensively and have had little to no paranormal activity at Fort Matanzas (the Castillo de San Marco, St. Augustine's other fort is another story see Historic Haunts Florida). Whether the green lights on the Matanzas can be explained as "will-o'-the-wisps" or ignited collections of methane swamp gas is uncertain. What is certain is that the frequently reported bloody red waters of the Matanzas are a lot harder to explain. Fort Matanzas and the waters that run alongside her have certainly been affected by the bloody period in Spain's history and America's past. A period that even now seems to have left paranormal repercussions.

THE SPIRITED GHOSTS OF THE SEA AND SUN

House of Sea and Sun, St. Augustine

House of Sea and Sun

This beautiful beach front home was built by Louise Wise Lewis Francis in the 1920s. She was the heir and niece of Henry Flagler. It was designed for grand yet casual social gatherings with a beautiful view of the Atlantic Ocean.
During the 1930s the St. Augustine High School used the building for their annual prom night. Back in the 30s graduating classes were much smaller than they are today. The place is still a gathering spot, this time for guests of the House of Sea and Sun Inn.

Ghostly Tales of the Inn

When we arrived for our investigation, I chatted with Patty Steder, the owner of the inn, who also lives on location. Patty has owned the building since 1994. She has heard many paranormal accounts and has had literally dozens of her own experiences.
    The inn consists of six guest rooms and some are more active than others. "Molly's Room" seems to be one of the more active rooms and was named after Molly Wiley Louise, daughter of Louise (who passes away while they were kids). Molly and her brother Lawrence helped Flagler College as they got older in the 1960s helping to assure the campus remained beautifully restored and up and running.
    Many guests while staying in Molly's Room report frequently experiencing cold chills running up their spines for no known reason. Many believe Louise is searching for Molly. Molly passed away only a few years ago so maybe Louise is trying to reconnect with her daughter whom she hasn't seen since Molly was about 10 or 11 years old.
    Besides Molly's Room, there have been a variety of other paranormal reports made

73

describing incidents in other parts of the inn. Some guests have reported hearing the sound of china clinking together, almost like a tea set bumping together on a tea tray. This occurs when no one and no items are in the room. Others have reported smelling an electrical smell on the staircase. I experienced this myself when entering the place. The owners claim the wiring has been checked repeatedly and are baffled by this phenomenon.

The Safari Room is another paranormal hot spot. Guests wake up in the night hearing music, dancing, and laughter as if prom night is still going on. As soon as they go to get up and see where it is coming from, all the sounds stop.

The paranormal incidents at the House of Sea and Sun are not just found inside the inn, but commonly occur on the grounds as well. On one occasion when guests were returning late one night after an evening out, they approached the mail door of the inn and saw two figures through the window in the door. They took a photo and captured the image. Unfortunately I do not have access to that photo, but Patty stated that she has it somewhere in her collection. Other guests have reported seeing the same image through the glass without knowing of the background of this incident.

In several other accounts guests saw an elderly woman rocking in a rocking chair on the porch but when they tried to approach the woman, she disappeared. Others have seen the same female apparition sitting in the breakfast room.

The mirror in the breakfast room

Our Investigation

During our investigation we were also told about an antique mirror in the breakfast room. We did catch some very strange EMF readings off this mirror and as soon as we moved the meter away from the mirror, the readings dropped back to 0. It also gave us a colder temperature reading. There were no breezes coming through the windows, the air conditioning wasn't on, and no other circulating air conditions were present to explain the temperature drop.

Patty told us that when the ghosts get too rowdy she just tells them to stop and they do. She backed this up by recounting an example of an event that happened when a large group of girls with a wedding party stayed the night. They were loud, rude, and drunk and the ghosts didn't like what was going on in "their" house. The spirits would turn on the cold water when they were trying to take hot showers, or turn the blow dryers off when the girls tried to dry their hair. In some cases the spirits just completely shut the power off. This made enough of an impact on the ladies to change their behavior and practically scared them sober.

During our investigation all was quiet for the most part.We didn't pick up on anything substantial with our equipment and had packed up. It wasn't until the middle of the night (around 4 a.m.) when I was woken up by the sound of furniture being moved around on the upstairs hallway. I went to see what was going on and the sounds stopped. After a quick look around I learned that I seemed to be the only one up in the house.

We did use the Ovilus III during our investigations but didn't capture any words that made any sense. I don't agree 100% with this piece of equipment but do use it from time to time to see what it comes up with or what it might stir up.

This beautiful and haunted inn is most definitely worth an overnight stay while in St. Augustine. Its so very peaceful and so are the ghosts, provided that you respect their space. We were happy to be allowed to experience and investigate this spirited place.

SOPHIE'S CHOICE
Peace and Plenty Bed and Breakfast, St. Augustine

*The sign marks the popular
Peace & Plenty*

The Peace and Plenty Inn was built in 1894 by German, Conrad Decher. He and his much younger wife, (25 years to be exact) Sophie Emilie, lived here for many years during the social seasons (January through March). Conrad and Sophie never had any children but Conrad did have some from a previous marriage. Many of those children referred to Sophie as Conrad's trophy wife.

Decher made his money in Boston on real estate deals. He left Boston when he was 58 for St. Augustine where he owned St. Augustine & South Beach Railway and Bridge Company. He also had business connections with Rockefeller and Flagler, and built the first Bridge of Lions for his train line to service the beach area.

The Peace and Plenty moves on

Decher passed away in 1907 when he was 78 years old. There is some disagreement over whether he passed at the Railroad Hospital on King Street or in the house itself. Most believe he passed away in the house and (as most people did in those days) that the wake and funeral were held in the front parlor. When the funeral was over, Decher was taken out the "funeral door". Many Victorian homes had these doors and it is (basically just a reference to the back door). Sophie would go on to have a daughter named Elizabeth, before she too passed away in the house in 1935. Her wake and funeral were also held in the front parlor before she left the home through the funeral door. (Or did she?) Elizabeth would have a daughter of her own, and that woman would go on to marry a man named Walter Decker. The obviously similar names have ever been explained, nor their possible connections traced.

The house itself was subdivided in the 1970's and served as apartments to Flagler College Students. it was purchased by Court Terrell and his mother Glenna in 1996.

During the restoration of the house the owners found a hidden staircase behind some dry wall and the story was featured on HGTV's, "If Walls Could Talk". They also encountered a message on which was written "this room was made by Walter Decker in July 1937". Further investigation yielded the fact that a child's room had once existed under the stairs, and that three rooms were rented out during the Depression to provide extra income. Court and his mother completed their interior renovations in 2000. As is sometimes the case Renovations of this type are believed to stir things up a little in the paranormal sense, and the owners have certainly been experiencing this first hand.

Investigating the Peace and Plenty

Historic Haunts Investigations was invited to investigate this beautiful Victorian gem in December of 2012. The owners described some personal experiences they've had and remarked that apparently Sophie loves what has been done to HER home. However, she only seems to interact with guests in the room at the top of the staircase. That is where our investigation began.

We set up all of our equipment, but unfortunately didn't get any responses to any of the questions or equipment. There were simply no fluctuation in readings, sounds, movement, or anything else. We decided to turn in for the night since it seemed Sophie didn't want to talk with us. I left the camera running and the K2 EMF Meter was still out I asked, "Sophie, can you at least show me yourself in my dreams tonight?" After asking my question the K2 meter flickered slightly. I took that as a yes and went to bed. As I settled into bed the bathroom door closed on its own accord. Gayel, a member of my investigation team got up from her bed at the same time I got up from mine, we walked over and tried to recreate the experience. The door would not budge, using any reasonable or rational means, and the door was not situated so as to have this occur naturally once opened at least to us. Still uncertain, we closed the bathroom door and went back to bed. Once again we settled in and the door opened. We got back up, walked around, jumped in front of the door, created a breeze, and still got no response, the door would not move. We investigated other potential causes, the heat or air hadn't kicked on or provided any means to cause a suction or a breeze. I moved the video camera to where it would face directly at the bathroom door. Gayel and I both went back to bed and nothing else happened as we fell back to sleep.

However, during the night I had a dream that I was standing at the front door of the house but in a different time. Everything looked like it was from the late 1920s or early 1930s. I knocked on the door and could see through a window in the door, a beautiful slender woman, about my size, started to descend the staircase. She had long dark hair which was pulled to the side and hanging down over her right shoulder. She was wearing a pale yellow dress and she had blue eyes. (I do dream in color).

The next morning when we got up we checked the video, the door never budged. I told Gayel about my dream and thanked Sophie out loud in case she had in fact come to me in my dream. I asked the owners if they had any photos of Sophie and was told they hadn't come across any yet. I am still looking to confirm whether the woman I viewed in the dream.

Peace and Plenty is a beautiful and warm place to stay in the heart of the nation's oldest city. The bed and breakfast is a luxurious getaway and a perfect romantic setting. If the thought of staying in a haunted location doesn't bring you here, the walled garden, elegant fountains, outdoor cigar lounge, luxurious amenities or gourmet breakfasts just might

THE ROMANTIC GHOST
OF THE DON CESAR
Don Cesar Hotel, St. Petersburg Beach

Photo: Author

In 1924 Thomas Rowe purchased 80 acres of *The beautiful Don Cesar* land in St. Petersburg to begin his dream project.

His dream was to build a pink castle. Indianapolis architect Henry Dupont and contractor Carlton Beard were hired to make his dream come true. Since his pink castle was being built on the beach they had to insure the hotel wouldn't sink into the shifting sand. Beard designed a floating concrete pad with pyramid shaped footers. On January 16th, 1928 Thomas Rowe opened the Don Cesar Hotel in St. Petersburg Beach. Rowe named the Don Cesar after a heroic character from the opera Maritana. His Gatsby era hotel quickly enjoyed popularity as a playground among the famous and wealthy. Over 80 years later there are no signs of settling and the pink castle still shines in all her glory.

The reason for the Pink House

Thomas Rowe wanted his private home to look like the pink castle because that's where he had met the love of his life. While studying in London Rowe fell in love with a raven-haired beauty, a girl named Lucinda. She was an opera singer, and the two met on a regular basis. Her parents apparently didn't approve of their love as Rowe was a different religion and they sent her away never to see Thomas again. Rowe's letters were returned unopened (obviously screened by her parents). Rowe received one letter written by Lucinda just before she died apparently of a broken heart. In her letter she professed her love and lamented the fact that he had not written

78

her as promised.

When Rowe moved to America he vowed to never love another, he wanted to remember Lucinda by rebuilding the castle he met her in. He did enter into a loveless marriage with Mary Lucille Lowe whom he apparently left in Virginia after he received Lucinda's last letter from her parents. He moved to Florida at the age of 47 to build his hotel.

He died in 1940 and the hotel fell back under the control of his wife. She was not as good at maintaining a hotel and had little desire to do so. She eventually lost the property. During WWII the government owned the building and converted it into a VA hospital, in the process they stripped the hotel of many attractive elements (including the recreation of the fountain where Rowe met his beloved). They also bricked up windows, laminated over marble floors, and used the hotel's kitchen for a time as the morgue.

Eventually after the war, the hotel came under the control of the Lowe's Hotel chain. During this time it was also restored to resemble its once former glory.

Spirits of the Don Cesar

Thomas has been seen by many walking along the beach in his white suit looking out at the ocean or staring up at his beautiful castle. Others have seen him checking out the day to day operations of the hotel and greeting guests before vanishing. Some have even seen him walking hand in hand with his beloved Lucinda. He often times makes himself known to loving couples who are affectionate and walking along the beach or inside his old home which is now a luxurious hotel. Maybe they are finally together in the afterlife after all those years apart.

Besides the spirit of Thomas Rowe, there are other paranormal disturbances that many believe may be attributed to its time as a VA hospital. The lights have been known to flicker unusually in areas of the hotel. The electrical systems in these areas have been checked extensively and no explanation has been discovered. The kitchen has been the frequent victim of phantom noises and knocks and employees have claimed on several occasions to see the apparitions of nurses.

My Memories of the Don Cesar

I remember seeing this beautiful pink lady as a child when we went to the beach. I was always amazed by this place like it was just trying to draw me into it. Many people have reported feeling the same way when staying here and they are just in awe by its beauty. Maybe it is Thomas Rowe's way of acknowledging people's admiration to his dream castle? We may never know but if you see a well-dressed man wearing a hat and walking with a walking stick from days far gone around the property you can pretty much bet it is Mr. Rowe still walking the grounds keeping an eye on his home. Last time I was at the Don Cesar was in January 2011. As I walked St. Pete Beach totally alone, and looking up at this beautiful pink lady, I started talking out loud as if Thomas Rowe was there. I told him what a beautiful piece of work he had created and can see why he still lingers here. No sooner did I finish my sentence I caught something out of the corner of my eye. When I turned to look, it was gone. Could it have been the ghost of Thomas Rowe? I may have to go back and try it again so I can find out.

HASLAM'S BOOKS AND BOOS
Haslam's Bookstore, St. Petersburg

A Legacy of Literacy

John and Mary Haslam, both avid readers, started the Haslam Bookstore in 1933. They sold used magazines and books to help people who couldn't afford to buy and read new books. During the early days of the depression and the aftermath money was tight for many and the Haslam's wanted to keep reading alive and strong.

After World War II the second generation of the Haslam's family took over, Charles and Elizabeth. The store grew in customers and popularity. Ultimately, it ended up moving four times and finally expanded into the neighboring building in the 70's to make room for all the additional books the Haslam's offered.

Charles Haslam was such a devoted promoter of literacy and reading for fun that he had a television program on a local PBS station for 15 years called the "Wonderful World of Books". He also had a radio show for quite some time. He earned the nickname the "Bookman".

Haslam's is now over 30,000 square feet and contains over 300,000 books. It is said to be Florida's largest bookstore and one of the largest in the Southeast. In 1973, the third generation of the Haslam family took over, proudly carrying on the traditions and examples their grandparents set.

Haslam's Haunts

The paranormal accounts in this bookstore seem to have started during renovations and the expansion of the store. There have been many reports from customers who claim to feel someone behind them, as is often the case, when they turn to look and see who's there, they find no one. Many people reported being tapped on the shoulder by an invisible hand. The store itself seems to have areas and locations throughout where paranormal reports are more frequent and phenomenon more likely.
Books have been known to mysteriously fall over the book shelves. At Haslam's witnesses have described chilling cold spots in the center of an aisle (including the current manager/owner).

The Beat Goes On

Some believe the paranormal incidents can be attributed to the spirit of Jack Kerouac. He was a beat poet and writer who spent the last few years of his life in the St. Petersburg area. Kerouac was the iconic wandering voice of a restless Bohemian generation. He unfortunately bled to death in St. Anthony's Hospital in St. Petersburg in 1969; another beloved author who'd drunk himself to death. Kerouac would often come in and move his books to a higher spot closer to eye level where he thought customers could see them better. This of course, ruined the Haslam's method of keeping the books in alphabetical order. His books have been known to rearrange or even relocate. There have even been reports of Kerouac's books (including "On the Road" and others) suddenly hitting the ground behind people even in different areas of the store. Curiously, these books strike the ground as if dropped so that the flat side would slap

80

against the floor (making the loudest and most attention getting noise), instead of spine out as a book falling from the shelf normally would. Apparently he is still trying to boost his sales.

Ironically enough, an increase in books and alphabetical rearranging have moved Kerouac's books to eye level, just where he liked them. Since this reshuffling the reported paranormal incidents involving his books have decreased. Regardless, whether you experience a ghost at Haslam Book Store or not it is an amazing spot for avid readers (and writers like me). I was born in St. Petersburg and Haslam's is a local icon. I recommend you grab a book from Haslam's and a Coke (my favorite) and head to the beach. That, to me, equals a perfect day! If Kerouac's spirit is still around, wanderer that he was, he can come too.

PHANTOM HORSE OF CELERY AVENUE
Celery Avenue, Sanford

Sanford, Florida at one time was the "Celery Capitol" of the nation and was covered with celery fields from one end of town to the other. For decades reports of Celery Avenue being haunted have surfaced. Most of these reports are believed to be tied to two burial sites.

The Mighty Steed

Local legend in Sanford claims that years ago, a blacksmith by the name of Sligh Earnest had a horse that stood "22 hands" tall and weighed 3200 pounds. When the horse died, Earnest needed a tractor to hall the horse's body away to bury him. He buried his trusty steed along Celery Avenue, but since the burial, the road has been widened and paved over.

At about the time of the death of Earnest's giant horse, many have reported seeing a ghostly phantom horse galloping down the road or alongside their cars. Witnesses describe it as being a dark color and transparent, always running at a great speed down the avenue, but sometimes its not alone. Occasionally the horse is seen being ridden by a Native American warrior. Which leads us to the second (and much older) burial site believed to be tied to Celery Avenue...

Putting Something Before the Horse

Another story about Celery Avenue involves the ghostly Native Americans spotted in the area. The Sanford area was known to be inhabited long ago by Native Americans. These indians in the area later to be known as Celery Avenue, not only lived and prospered here, but also buried their dead. Apparently when the Celery Avenue road was widened and paved it also went through a sacred Indian burial ground.

Since then there have been numerous reports of paranormal activity along Celery Avenue involving spirits described as Native Americans. Apparitions of ghostly indians have been spotted by many. Others in the area frequently describe an unnatural sense of being watched. On rare occasions these reports describe the ghostly semblance of an indian warrior mounted on horseback. Whether this is Sligh Earnest's prize steed is unknown.

I have been to the Sanford area numerous times and have not experienced either of these Celery Avenue phenomenon. However, it seems as though the restless spirits of the horse and the American Indians are unhappy that their graves have been desecrated, but, can you blame them? There are many cases of historic locations being destroyed in the name of progress. Still, the progress it seems sometimes turns these historic locations into true historic haunts. I hope to investigate these reports in more detail in the future. Until then, whenever I travel down Celery Avenue I'll keep listening for the sounds of hooves and the sight of a ghostly flowing mane.

THE HAUNTED HOUSE OF REFUGE
House of Refuge (Life Saving Station)
Gilbert's Bar, Stuart

The House of Refuge is on the National Register of Historic Places and is one of the original ten houses of refuge on the Florida coast, the oldest structure in Martin County, and the only refuge house still standing. The place is considered a community icon and a testament to maritime heritage and humanitarian service.   It also has a long history of providing refuge to the living and apparently the dead.

A History of Providing Refuge

In 1876 the US Life Saving Service constructed ten "houses of refuge" or life saving stations under direction of Sumner Kimball along the Atlantic Coast of Florida. These houses provided living space for a "keeper" and his family. Here they led a solitary existence with one mission.

It was built to find, rescue, and minister to the victims of Florida's dangerous reefs and shoals. These families would routinely walk along the isolated shores as far as possible in an effort to search for shipwreck victims and prevent them from perishing from starvation, thirst, or exposure.

In 1915, the U.S. Life-Saving Service merged with other entities to form the U.S. Coast Guard. Afterwards the House of Refuge at Gilbert's Bar became U.S. Coast Guard Station #207. Keeper Axel Johansen and his wife Kate stayed on duty and his title became surf man #1. Four other men were also stationed at the house. By World War I this crew of five had been increased by Home Guard members.

In 1942 a lookout tower was built and additional buildings were created to help safe guard the Treasure Coast from German U-Boats who torpedoed freighters off the coast. In 1945, the U.S. Government decommissioned the House of Refuge and it sat empty until 1953 when Martin County purchased it along with 16 acres for $168. The Martin County Historical Society formed in 1955 to protect the building and created a museum as a tribute to the history of the station.

The House of Refuge Comes Out of its Shell

At about the same time it became a refuge of another sort. Under the direction of Ross Witham, Marine Turtle Coordinator for the Florida Department of Natural Resources, the building became a refuge for sea turtles. Now the sea turtles (like the shipwreck victims before them) were reliant on the House of Refuge and its life-saving measures.

Haunts of the House of Refuge

There are at least three current resident haunts believed to be found at the House of Refuge. The first is thought to be connected to the area before the House of Refuge existed. Many believe the reason the land and building are haunted can be traced to an Indian tribe who lived there eight centuries ago. The apparitions of Indians have been seen throughout the area. The specific nature of these Indians is harder to distinguish.

83

The second apparition reportedly encountered is that of the life-saving men of the station, the keepers. With a wary eye toward the treacherous coastline, the spirits of long gone coastal guardians still seem compelled to keep watch and walk along the rocks. At least that's what the frequent paranormal incidents reported here would lead you to believe. Apparitions have appeared often and still seem to appear to this day, they are often described in detail by eyewitnesses.

The third ghost tied to the House of Refuge is attributed to a Mrs. Bessey, the wife of a former keeper. Her apparition is reported often, and the kitchen area of the building always seems to have the smell of freshly cooked beef stew. This occurs even when the room or stove isn't in use (it hasn't been operational since the 1940s). Cold spots are also reported in the building. It would seem Mrs. Bessey, like the other keeper's wives before her, considers this refuge her home.

To this day it seems this Gilbert's Bar favorite is not only a place of refuge for the sea turtles struggling to survive, but also the deceased struggling to remain.

GHOST TIGER ON THE PROWL AT LOWRY PARK ZOO
Lowry Park Zoo, Tampa

Tampa's Lowry Park Zoo

Lowry Park Zoo was the first city zoo and consisted of about 56 acres. While it was originally in a smaller area, the decision was made to move and it opened in its current location in 1957. Lowry Park shares space with Fairyland, a park which concentrates on nursery rhymes, mazes and oak trees (and which has reminded me of Munchkin Land since I was a little kid).

Lowry Park's Progress

In desperate need of repairs in the early 1980s, Lowry Park closed for a time and underwent major renovations. It reopened in March 1988. There was little of the old zoo still recognizable, but among the many improvements was a hospital for injured Florida Manatees so that they can be rehabilitated and reentered into the wild.

In 2006 a female Sumatraz Tiger named Enshala slipped through an unlocked gate and terrified people while she prowled the zoo. They tried to tranquilize the tiger to no effect. Its been suggested that perhaps the excitement and adrenaline of the situation was counteracting the sedatives. As she tried to lunge after the zoo veterinarian, the direc-

Enshala in her prime

85

tor of the zoo made the difficult decision to shoot and kill the tiger before anyone was seriously injured.

Lowry's prowling ghost

Some people say that Enshala's spirit still roams the park. People have frequently caught something moving out of the corner of their eye that had markings and similarities to this amazing animal, but when they turn to look whatever was there is gone.

Recently I spoke with a former Lowry Park Zoo animal keeper who shared a few interesting stories with me.

He told me after the accident the keepers always had to work in pairs to double check each other's work making sure all gates were secure. In addition, he said there were several times when employees would be working in a back area where guests are not permitted after hours. It was at these times that he and other employees of the zoo would encounter Enshala's ghost. He would catch something dart by with the size and markings of the cat. He would turn to whomever he was working with and they would claim to have seen the same thing. Mysteriously, when they went to inspect the area they saw the large mass dart too, there would be nothing there and nowhere for it have escaped to.

After all the years working at the zoo the ex-keeper also told me how you get to know the different sounds that each individual animal makes by heart. He knew Enshala well and knew all the sounds this particular cat would make. He said one day while working in the tiger area he distinctly heard the tiger behind him, he said it sounded like Enshala purring. When he turned around there was no Enshala and no cats to be found anywhere nearby.

The ex-keeper also informed me that other employees had reported seeing or hearing things, but were scared to tell anyone else about it because of the possibility of losing their jobs. Maybe Enshala is still roaming the zoo. Probably wondering why she's in the state she's in. The zoo hosts an annual Halloween event called Zooboo, but incidents of attendees spotting Enshala have been scarce at best. This tiger who for the most part grew up at the zoo and with the city, still seems to get around the zoo it called home for many years

THE SPIRITED TAMPA THEATRE
Tampa Theatre, Tampa

The Tampa Theatre opened on October 15th, 1926 and during its hay day was known as one of America's most elaborate movie palaces. It took one year to build and was designed by architect John Eberson. It's a Florida Mediterranean design and look took $1.2 million to construct.

Tampa's Movie Palace
Opening night was only .25 cents per person and the first movie shown here at the theatre was a silent film entitled "The Ace of Cads" starring Adolph Menjou. Patrons were treated as royalty when visiting here enjoying some of the most amazing movies and performances.

By the 1960s and 1970s times were changing and people were relocating to the suburbs which caused the attendance to decline greatly. Many of

The lights of Tampa Theatre

these grand movie palaces closed or demolished. Before this happened to the Tampa Theatre locals rallied yo save their historical gem.

In 1973 the theatre closed and stayed that way for several years until the city raised enough money to start the restoration process. When the theatre reopened in 1978 it had become a national example for how to save endangered theatres across the country.

The community continues to support the theatre and keep it alive and thriving. The ghosts seem to keep the movie palace running as well.

The ghosts of Tampa Theatre
One of the spirits who still resides here worked at the theatre in the 1940s. This young man absolutely loved his job. He worked at the theatre until his death. He worked in the projection room then entire time he was employed here and apparently continues to do so in his afterlife.

People have reported to me that they have heard footsteps heading to the projection room and then hear or would even see the door open and close while no one was there. Further, after they heard and saw the door close they would hear the sounds of

87

someone moving around in the projection rooms as if they were prepping a movie to be shown. These sounds included canisters being moved around and even the projector operating. Witnesses claim it they went to the projector room and opened the door, there would be no one there and the projector wouldn't be moving either.

Another report is an icy cold draft that causes the hair on the back of one's neck to stand on end. People have reported the sense of someone walking behind them, just before the icy cold chill would be felt. Witnesses claim they would turn around and find no one was there.

This is a beautiful old theatre and the gentleman that still haunts it must really love his job, and that is the type of job we would all love to have. He seems to keep doing it even in his afterlife.

HOW SOUTHERN BELLES AND LEGO BLOCKS FIT TOGETHER

Cypress Gardens, Winter Haven

One of Cypress Garden's botanical walkways

On January 2nd, 1936, Dick Pope Sr. and his wife Julie opened a botanical garden in Winter Haven Florida called Cypress Gardens. Over the years it became one of the biggest attractions in Florida, known for its water ski show, gardens, and southern belles. They had lovely young ladies in southern belle style dresses sitting throughout the gardens. Later it became known as the "Water Ski Capital of the World".

Through the years it saw several different owners and had been revamped many times. Then in 2004, after great renovations it became Cypress Gardens Adventure Park trying to compete with the larger theme parks in Central Florida. The triple Hurricane Roller Coaster was added and was names after Charley, Frances, and Jeanne, the three hurricanes that hit earlier that year.

As time passed and the Orlando theme park scene kept growing, Cypress Gardens slowly died off as did other smaller theme parks in years past. The company filed for bankruptcy in 2009, by September it shut its gates for the final time. The area that was once known as Cypress Gardens is now, after major renovations and construction, Legoland.

Haunts of the Former Cypress Gardens

I had the opportunity to interview one of the current employees of Legoland who also used to work there when it was Cypress Gardens. While there are several I interviewed who had knowledge of the ghosts of Cypress Gardens, she was the only one

89

who would step forward and discuss it (under conditions of anonymity). She reported that when she worked at the gardens seeing a transparent woman in a southern belle dress walking the gardens and around the gazebo was not uncommon. The spirit never interacted with her, she said it was like the apparition didn't even know she was there watching her. The spirit just seemed to walk through the gardens, up to the gazebo, and disappear. The former C.G. now Legoland employee said other people reported seeing it too, but were cautious to talk about it.

The stories of the transparent apparition leads me to believe that it is a residual haunt or residual energy and it just replaying the same thing over and over again. These residual haunts are like an impression on the atmosphere.

Apparently the southern belle is still there, at Legoland. This past employee told me several people reported seeing her when the gardens were still open and now people at Legoland are seeing her as well. Many people are still leery about discussing ghosts because they are afraid someone will think them to be crazy, or they worry they may lose their job. I can't blame people for needing to keep their jobs in this day and age when jobs are hard to come by, but I do wish places would be more open about their resident spirits and paranormal activity.

The stories of paranormal activity at the former Cypress Gardens does make you wonder.

Could the apparition of the southern belle be a former Cypress Gardens Belle who never wanted to leave, or is unaware that she has passed and just continues to do her job in the gardens. We may never know since she never interacts with the living but it is worth a visit to see the new park, remnants of the old park and possibly the southern belle along the way. Maybe while I'm there I can find some Lego Blocks and build a model of this Historic Haunt.

THE SMOKEY GHOSTS OF YBOR'S PAST
Ybor Factory Building, Ybor City

Ybor Factory Building

Ybor's Founding

In the heady days of the cigar industry demand for good hand-rolled cigars was a constant. Vincente Martinez-Ybor wanted to create a hub for cigar production and a place where his factories and workers could all be nearby one another. He brought in architect C.D. Parcell and was rewarded with several large buildings, globe street lights, wrought iron balconies, brick lined walkways, social clubs, and cigar factories, all with a distinct Latin feel. This new landmark district in Tampa would become known as Florida's Latin Quarter. Ybor would move his Principe de Gales "Prince of Wales" cigar line from Key West to the new building. Ybor's factory was three stories high and took up an entire city block (between 8th and 9th Avenue and 13th and 14th Street). Other cigar makers followed Ybor's lead and moved to the area, making Ybor City the Cigar Capitol of the World and Mr. Ybor's monolithic brick factory was the center piece. Ybor City at one time held over two hundred cigar factories which produced over seven hundred million cigars in a given year!

At Ybor's factories and others like it, the many Cuban, Italian, and Spanish immigrants became skilled Tabaqueros (cigar makers). Rolling their cigars everyday on wooden work benches and dealing with the conditions of the factories. Unfortunately, they also dealt with unhealthy living conditions in their casitas (homes) including angry alligators, disease infested waters, yellow fever, and infectious mosquitoes.

Mr. Ybor died in 1896 and the building went through a variety of owners, but it still continued making cigars until World War II. That's when the cigar industry

91

changed. Cigar production and demand began to decline during the Great Depression and many mafia and criminal groups slowly began taking over Ybor's streets, hotels, bars, and other fixtures. Charlie Wall, Florida's first crime lord was active in the area and shoot-outs between the police and Charlie's Crew were a common occurrence. The Ybor factory building situated among all these economic changes sat vacant for many years and was later used in the 1970's as a Gallery and studio for artists, called Ybor Square . In 1972 it was added to the US National Register of Historic Places.

In 2002 it was converted into offices except for the Spaghetti Warehouse. Then in 2010, the entire complex was bought by the Church of Scientology.

Ybor's Haunted History

Even though the build-ing is now owned by a church it still seems to house the spirits of some of the workers from the cigar factory. Ybor City in general seems to be filled with ghost stories through-out, including tales in many locations of ghosts riding elevators and wan-dering Ybor's hallways. Many people believe these spirits to be intelligent haunts of workers from the cigar era or men murdered during Ybor's darker crime-riddled past. In most cases people report hear-ing ghostly conversations spoken in Spanish coming

The building's current owners

from completely empty rooms. Typically Spanish-speaking men will be heard at the end of hallways, but upon inspection, witnesses find themselves completely alone.

Despite the fact that you can't tour the factory building now, while in Ybor city, make sure you walk by and catch a glimpse of this piece of Ybor's haunted history.

NOTES ON EQUIPMENT
Historic Haunts Investigations
....

Where we get our gear...

Many people ask me about the equipment I use during my investigations and where I get it. Historic Haunts Investigations uses cameras from Gotcha Ghost and have been doing so for years. Their cameras are high quality and light weight at a reasonable price. We have captured some amazing footage using their cameras and will continue to do so.
www.ghosthuntingcamera.com

When using these fantastic cameras, we need lights to get out best shots. We get our infrared, UV, and full spectrum lights from Phantom Lites. They have so many options when it comes to lights; they are one of the best in the field. You can virtually find a light for any type of camera your group uses.
www.phantomlites.com

When it comes to equipment, we almost always deal with Ghost Hunters Equipment/GhoSt Augustine. They have equipment for beginners who are just exploring the field to high tech pieces for the well experienced. They can complete your ghost hunting arsenal so you are prepared for any investigation.
www.ghosthuntersequipment.com

ABOUT THE AUTHOR

Jamie Roush Pearce

Jamie was born in St. Petersburg, Florida. After several unusual encounters at historic sites as a child, Jamie developed a passion for history and the paranormal. She began to research and investigate paranormal sites and stories. She established Historic Haunts Investigations in 2004 to display her research and findings, and provide an outlet where others could share their stories.

She continued her studies in Parapsychology under noted authority in the field Loyd Auerbach. She has gone on to be featured on the cable tv show ***Most Terrifying Places in America*** and has been proudly featured in several newspaper articles. To this day she continues researching the paranormal, counts several note-worthies in the field as peers and friends, and has even been present at the taping of several shows by famous televised ghost hunting groups.

Jamie was happy with the warm welcome her first book **Historic Haunts** received (now on it's third printing) and has eagerly been working on the sequels. She has been a contributor to The Florida Times Union, Jacksonville Magazine as well as other Florida publications. She continues to post the evidence of her investigations and research of the paranormal through her website **www.historic-haunts.net** and with her team **Historic Haunts Investigations.** She lives in Florida with her husband Deric, her living cat Griffin and the spirit of her deceased kitty Cosmo. She is hard at work on more sequels and has enjoyed meeting fans recently at her first conventions, where she was also able to share her new found interest in Dr. Who.

Use the following pages to log your own paranormal experiences at the locations in the book or at others:

Made in the USA
Columbia, SC
09 October 2021

46960620R00059